KAWAII CAT
COLORING BOOK

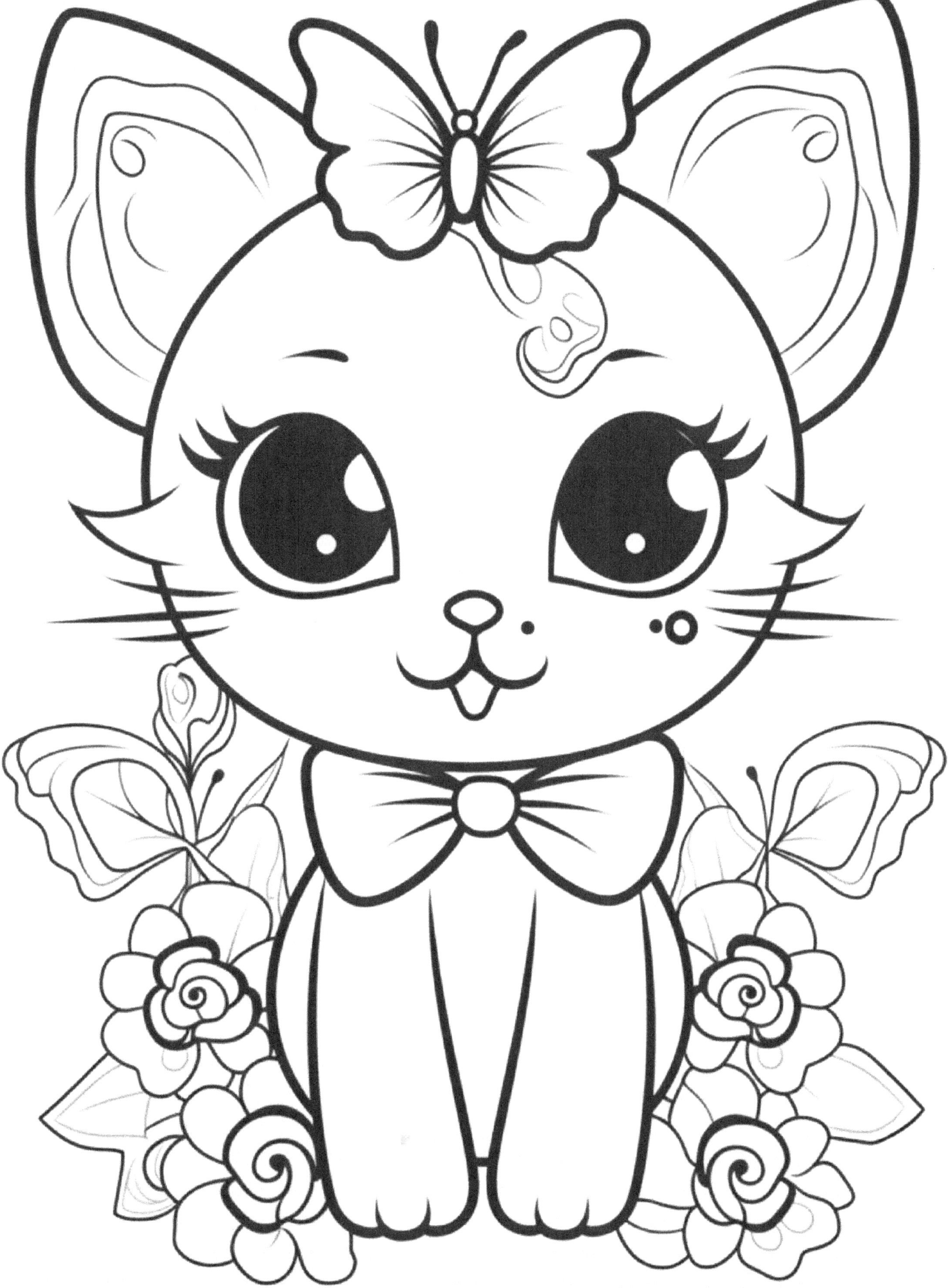

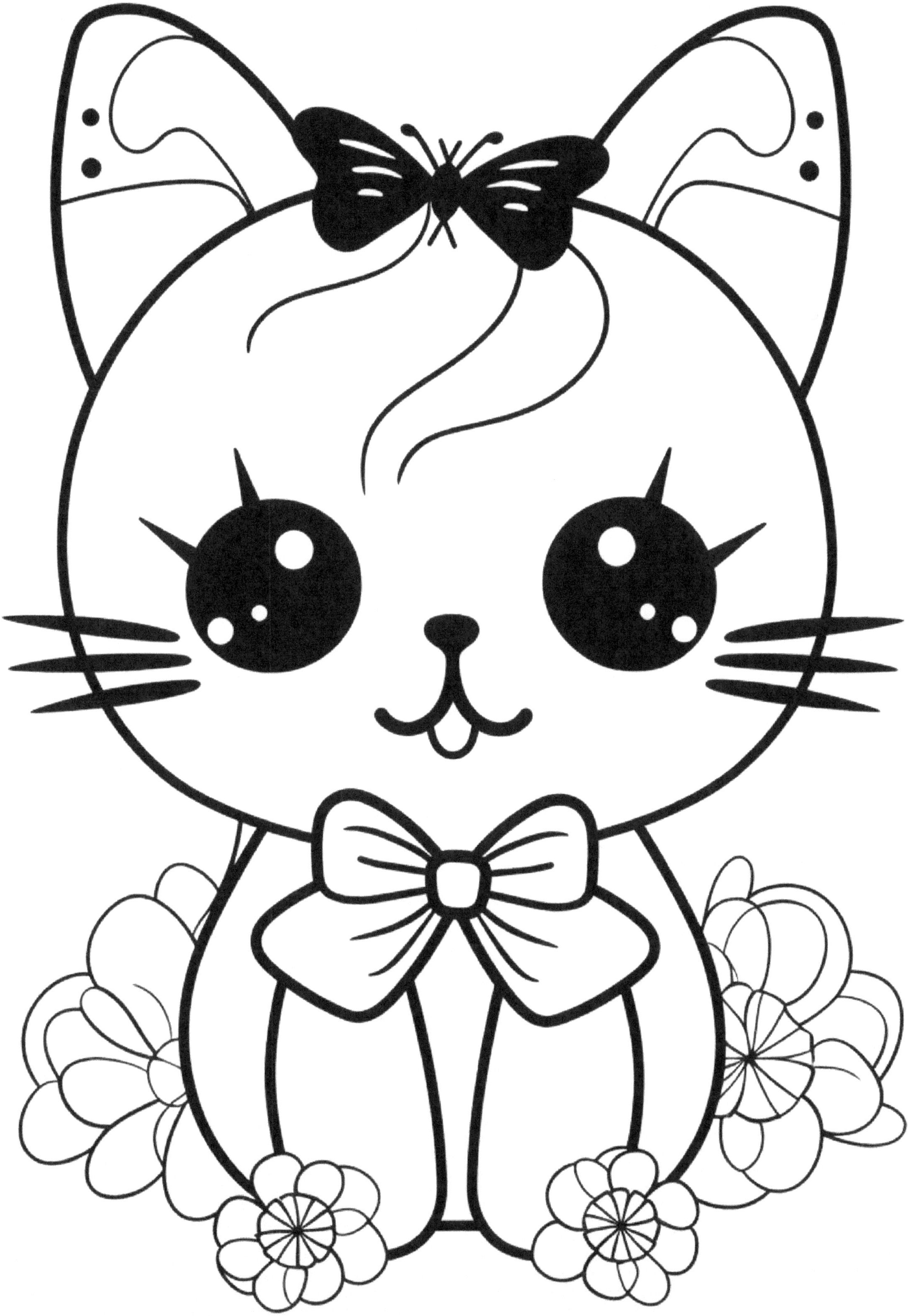

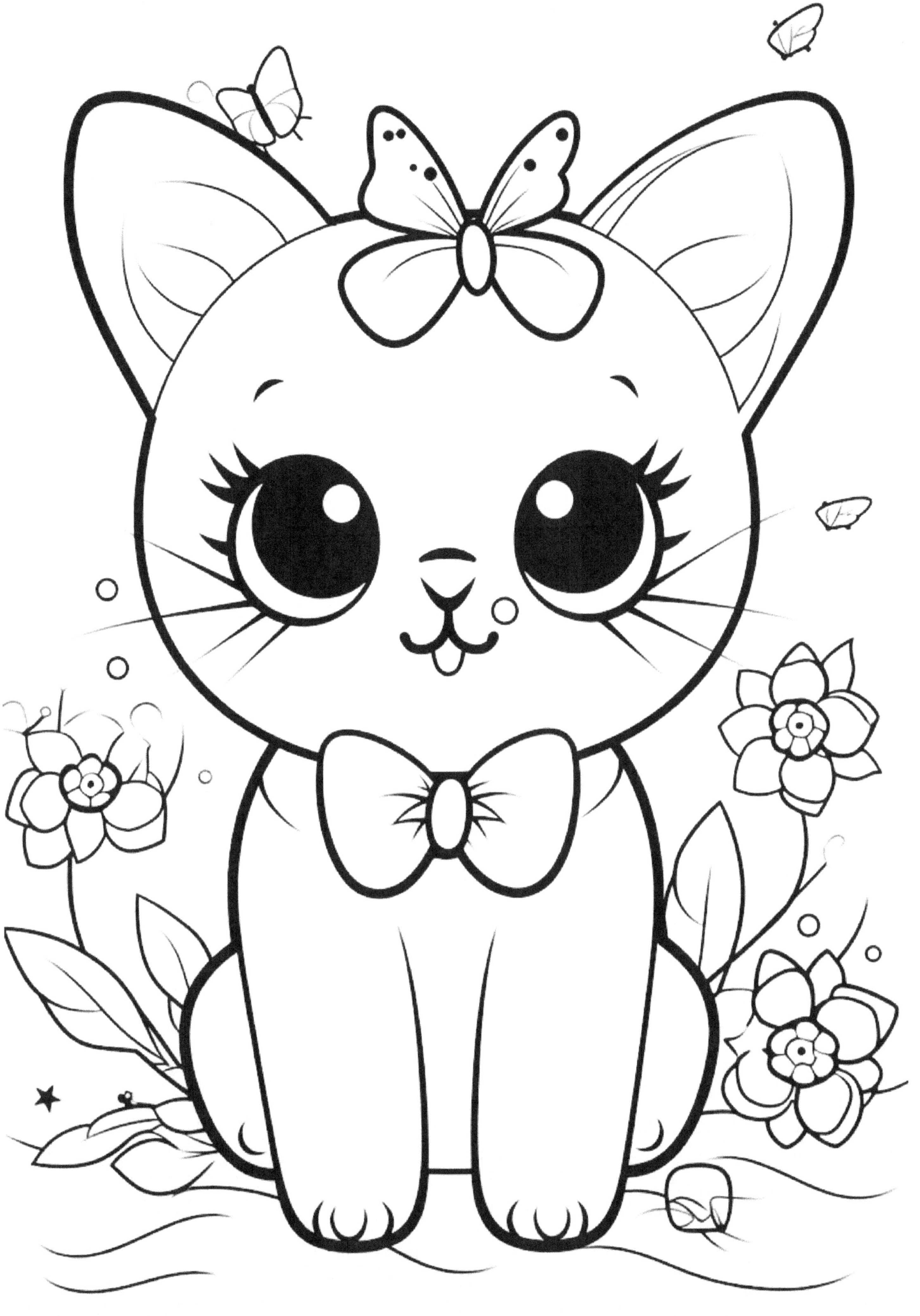

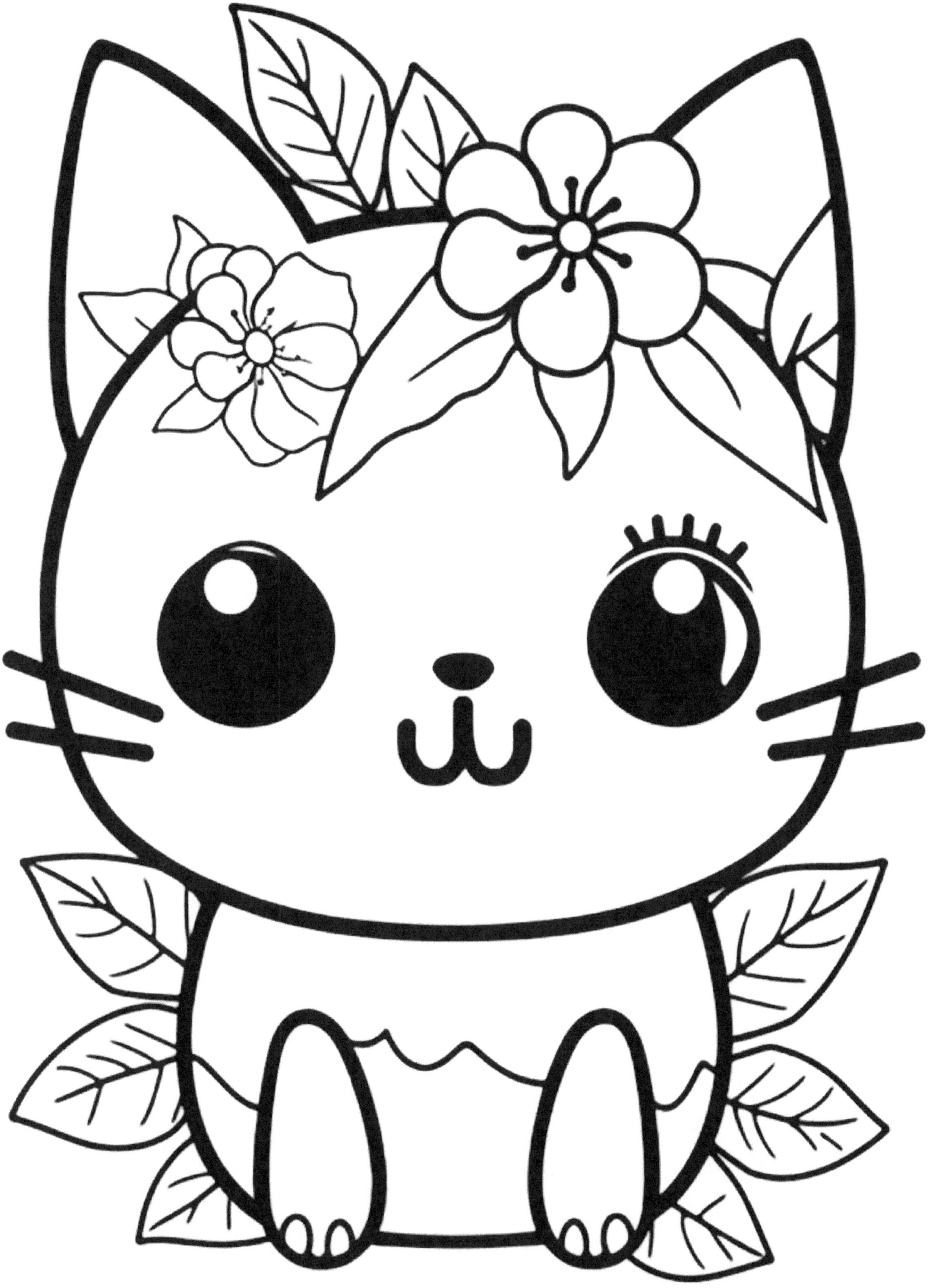

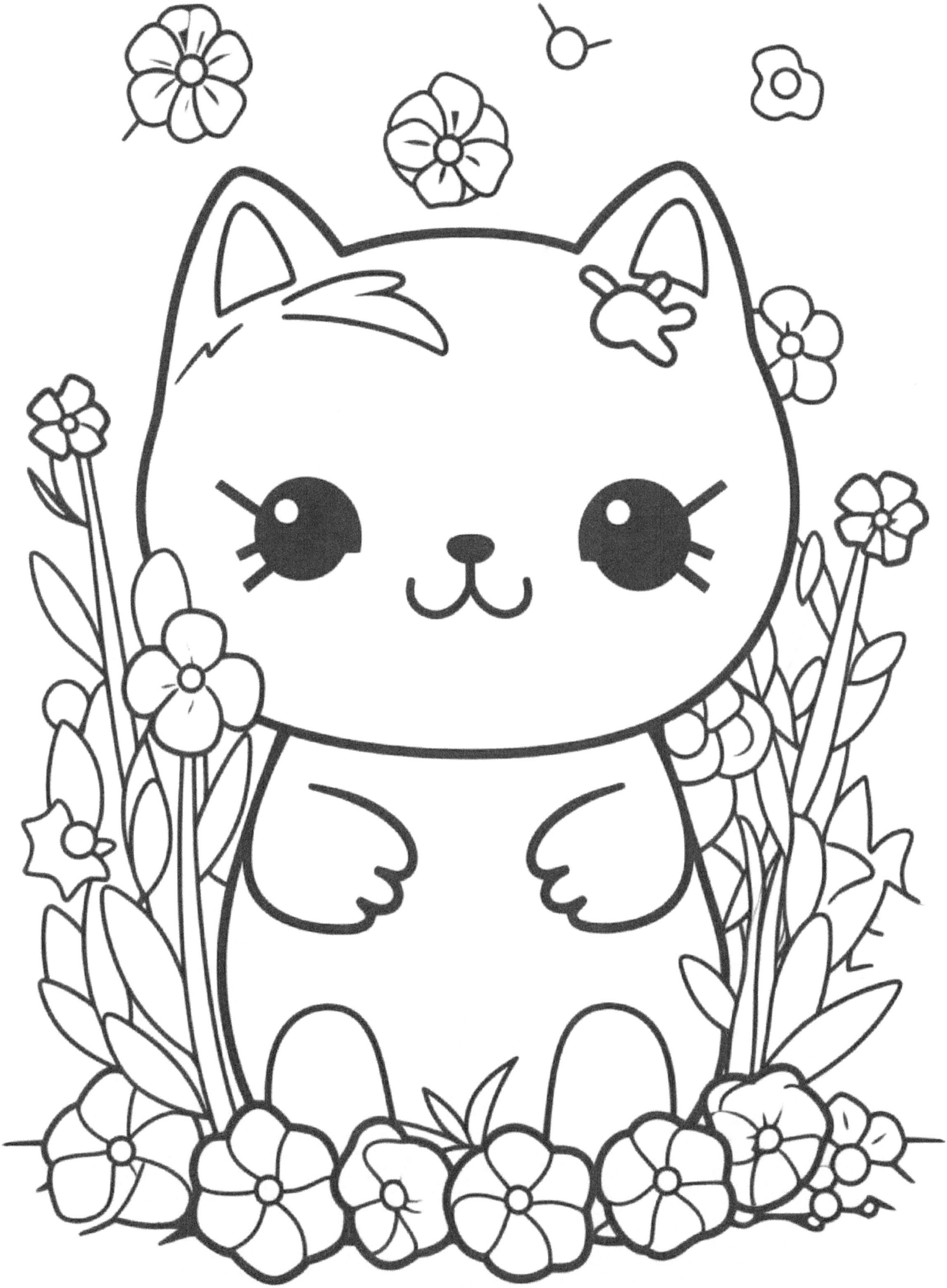

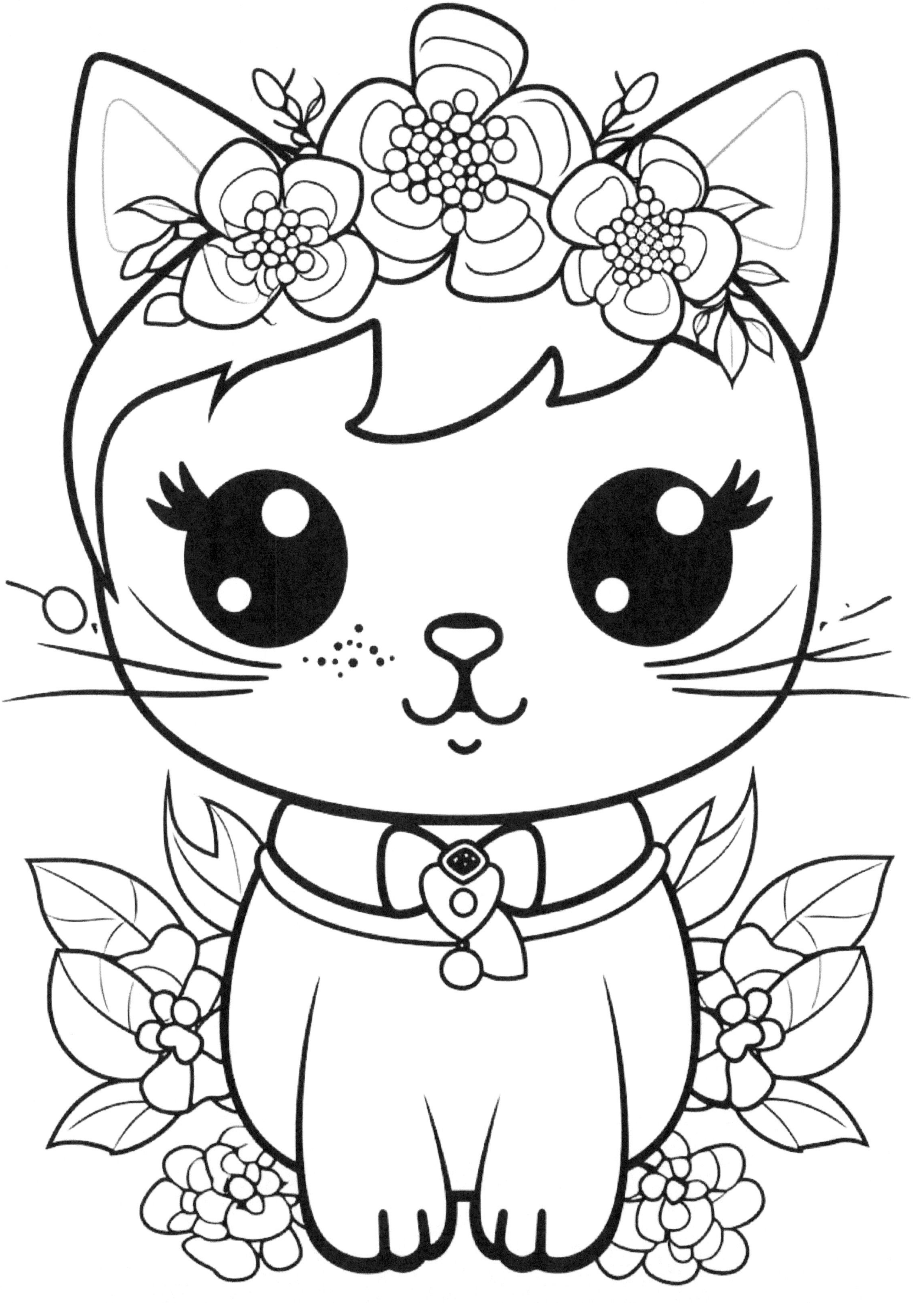

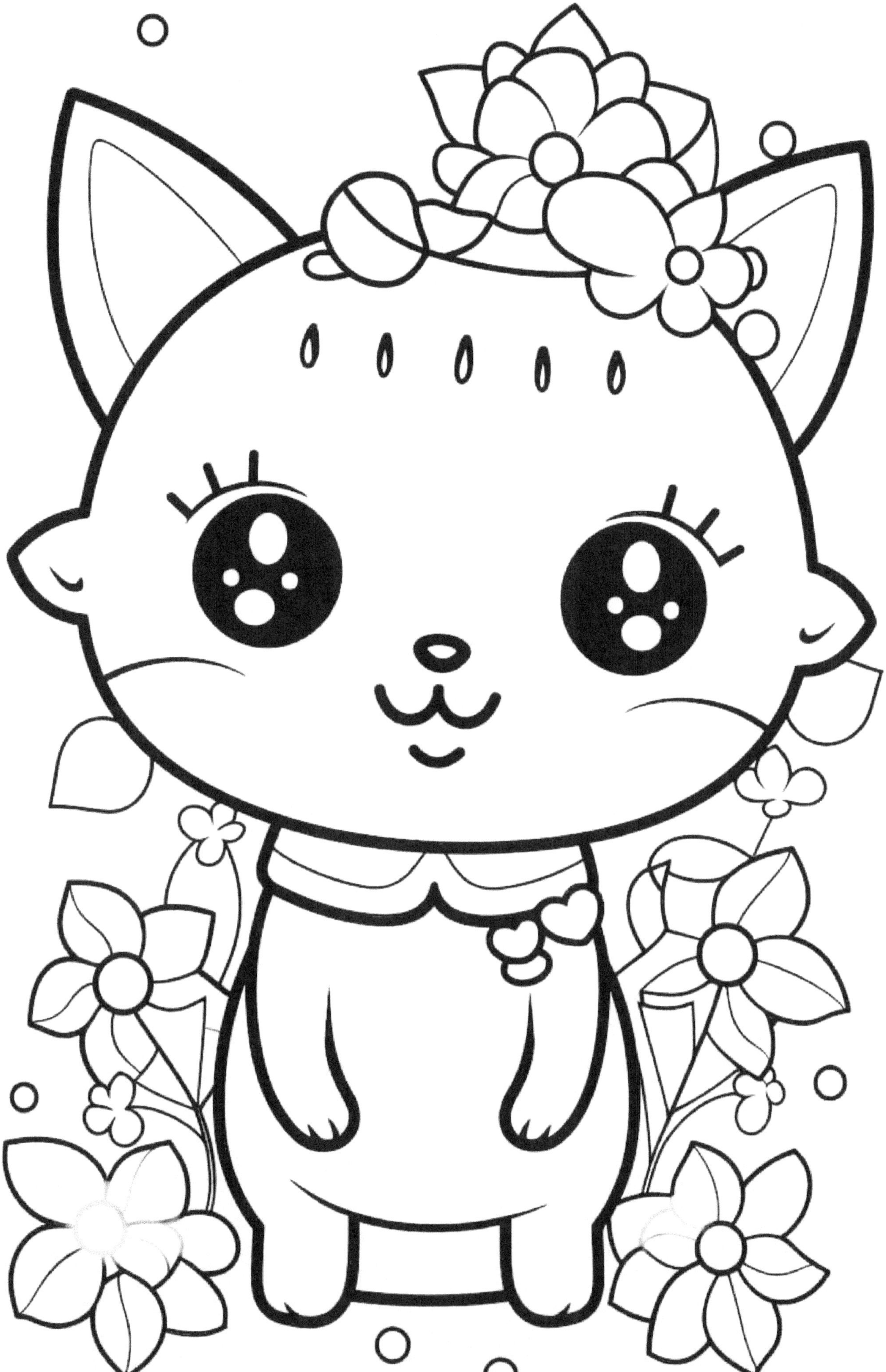

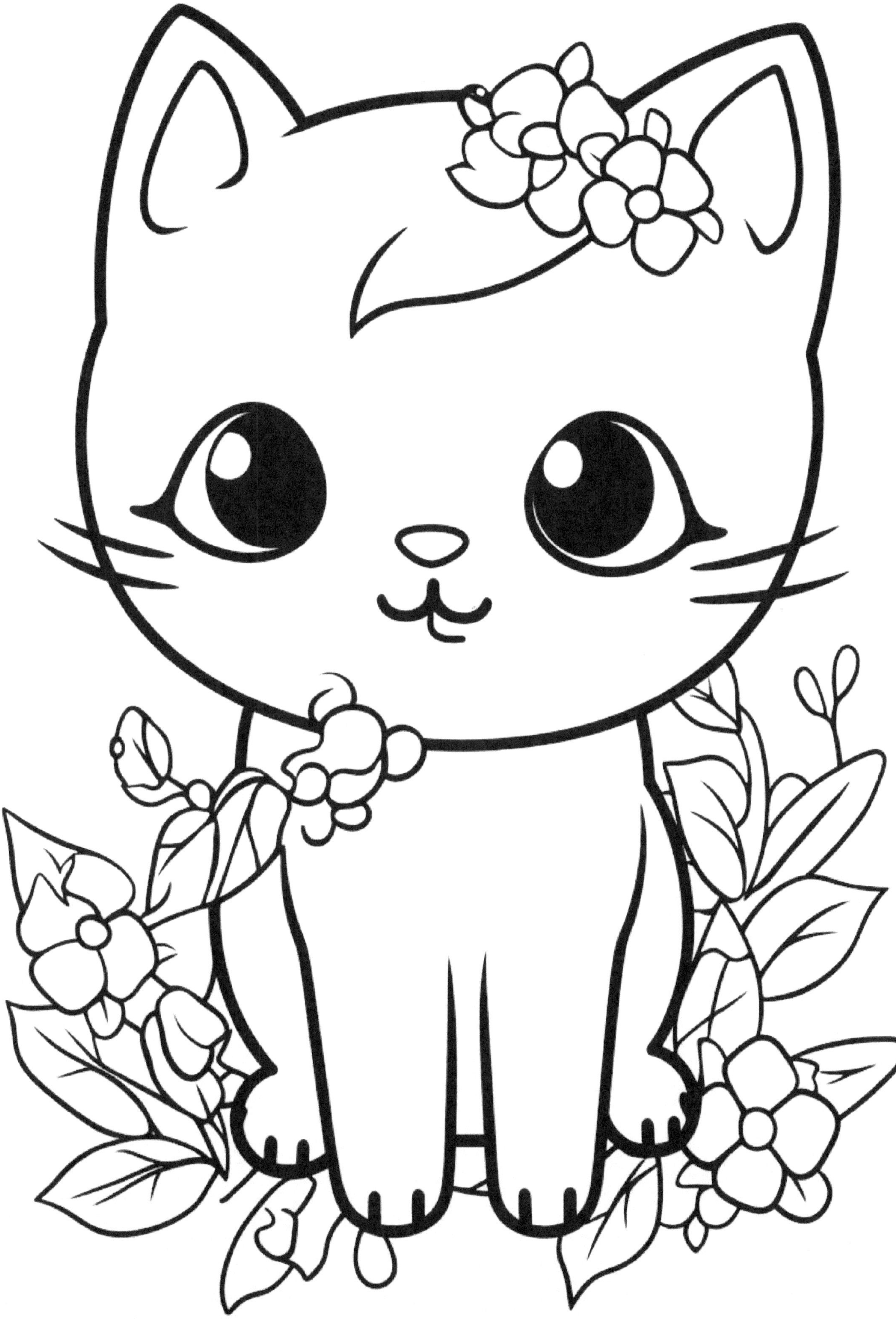

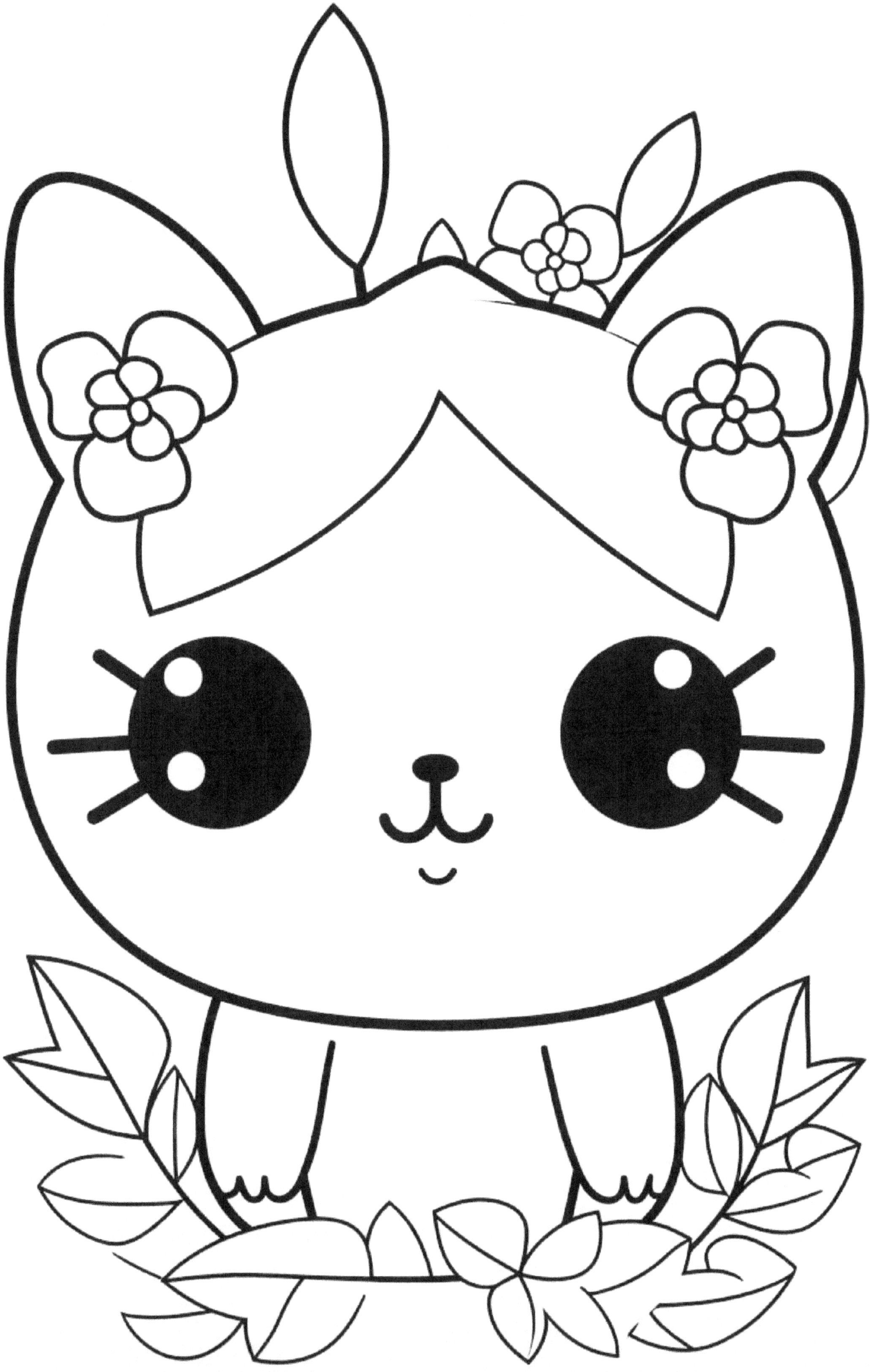

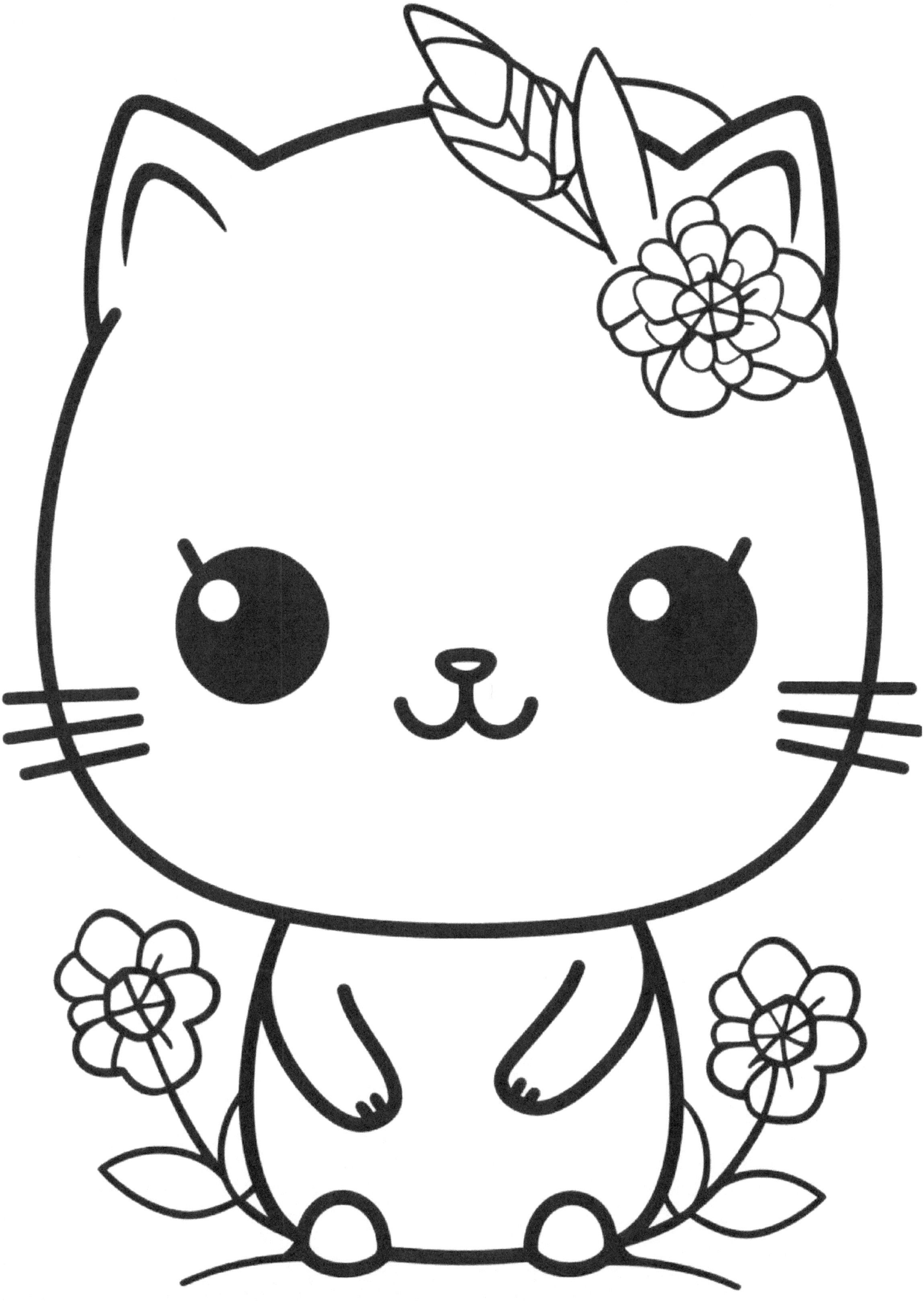

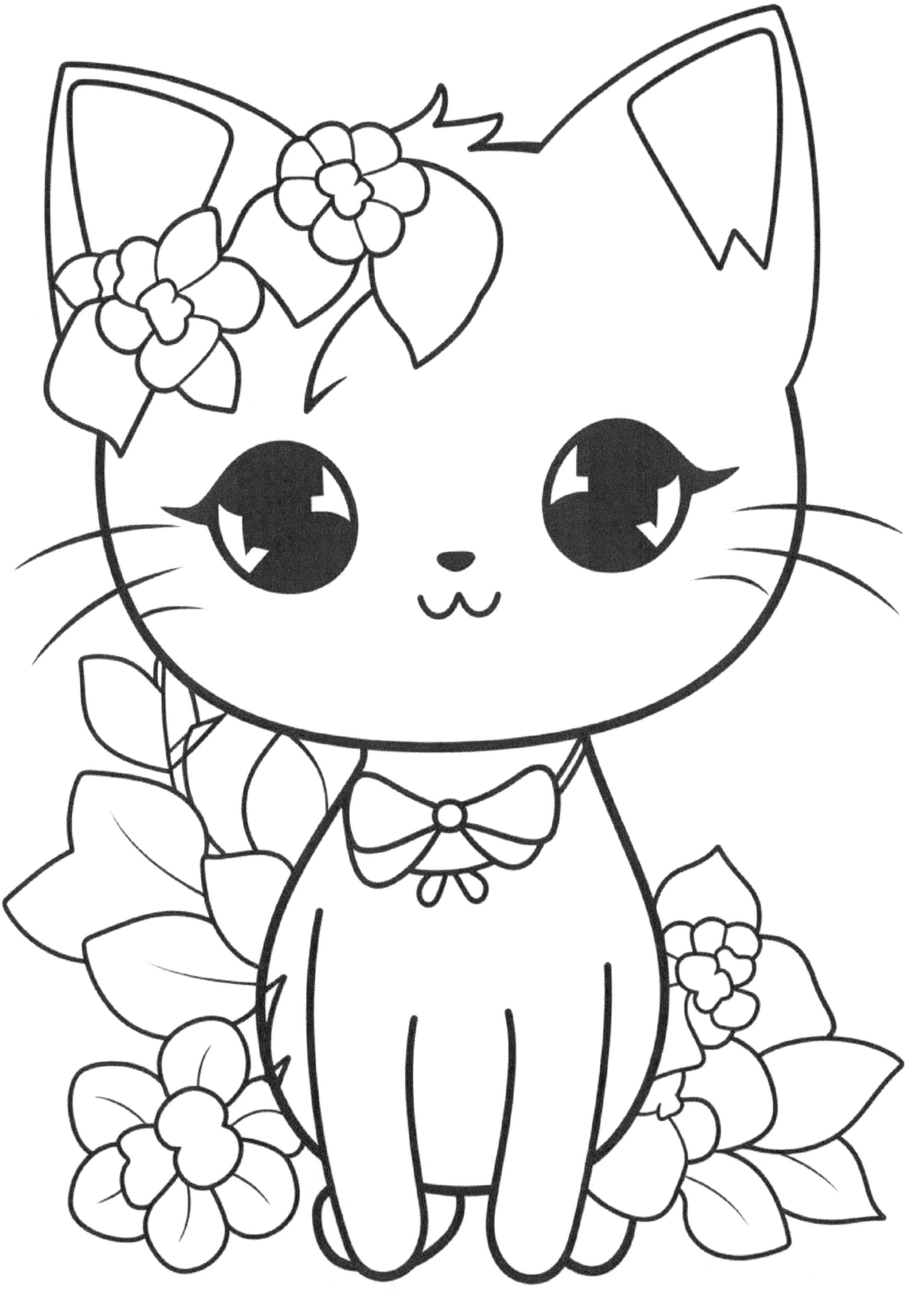

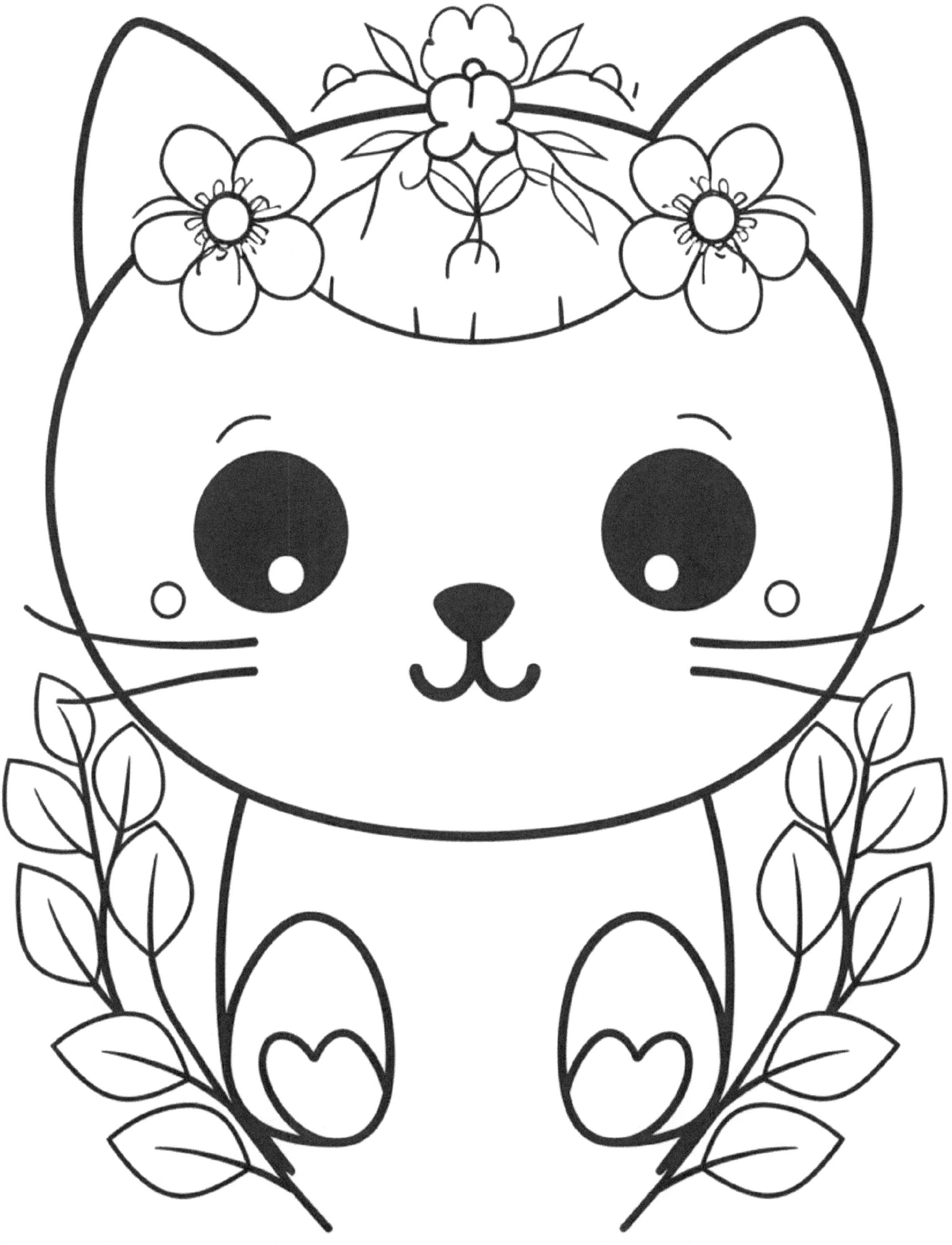

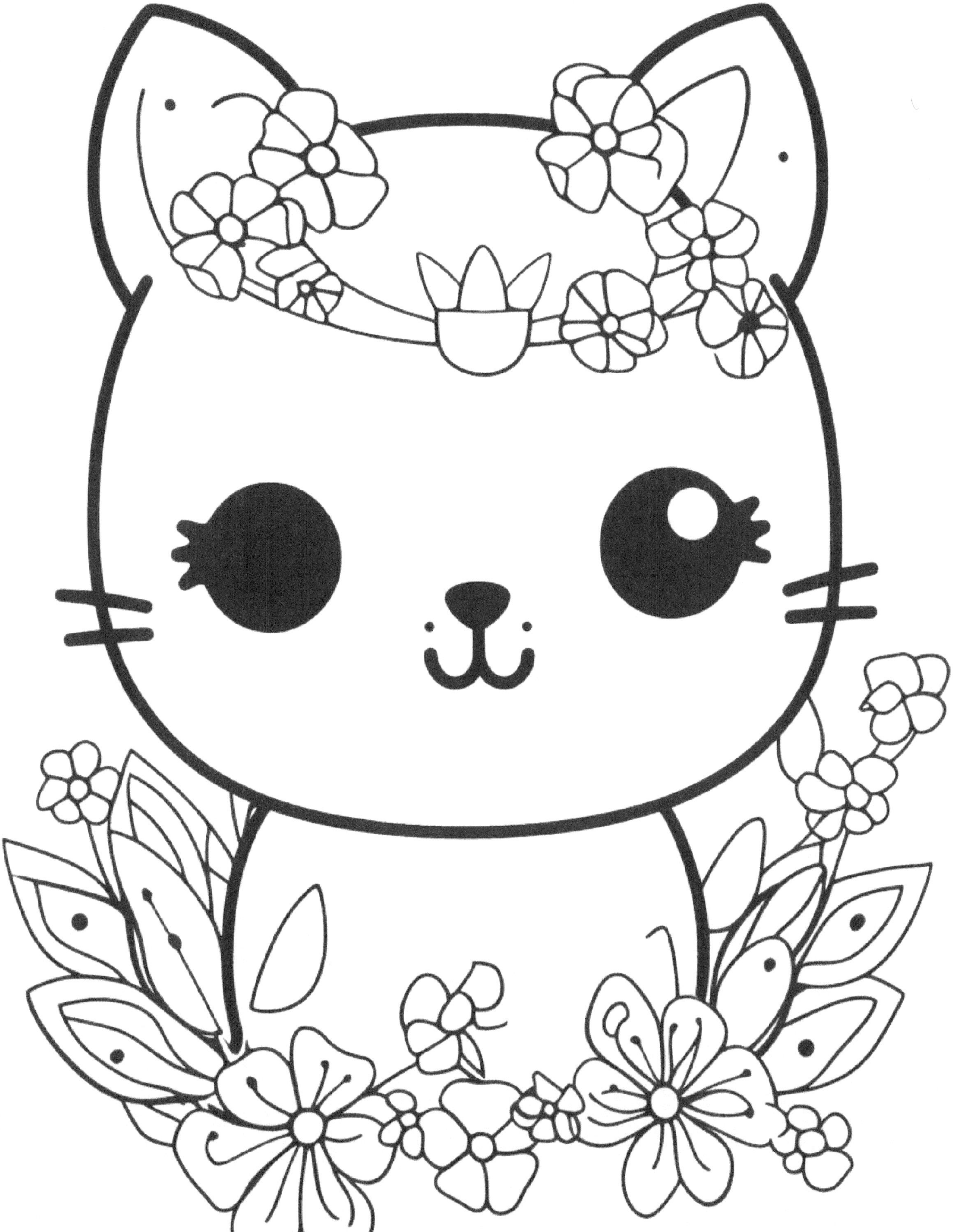

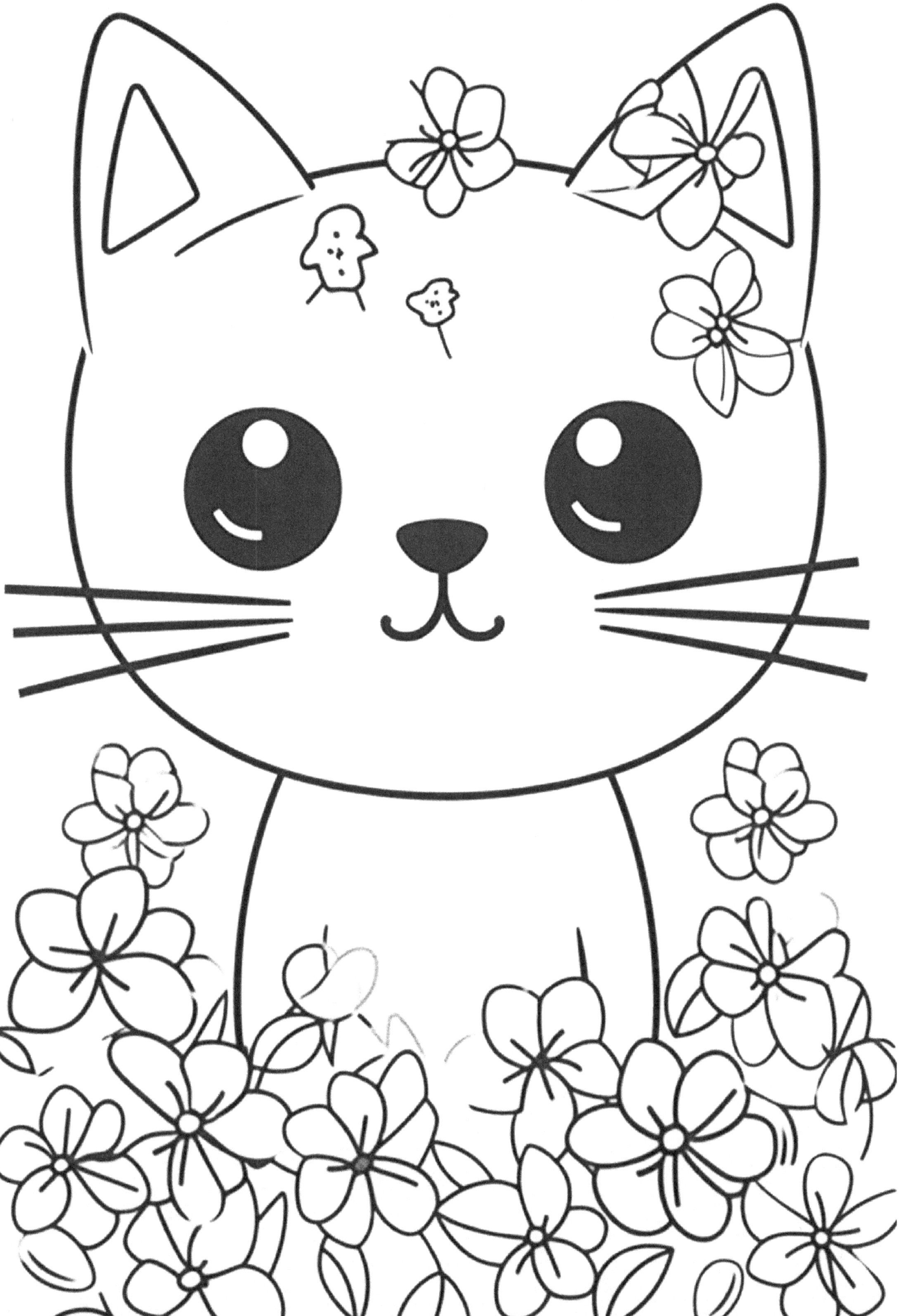

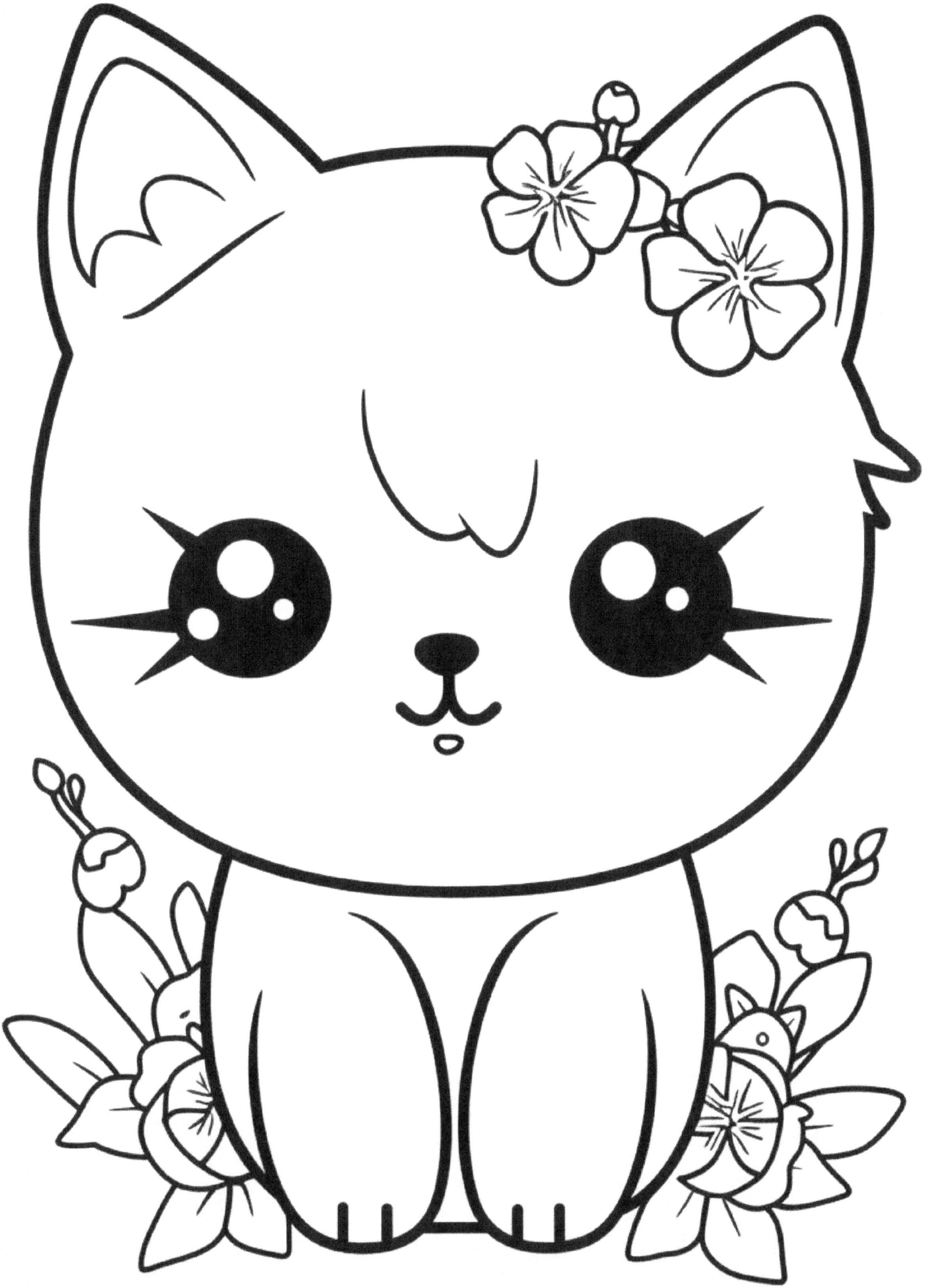

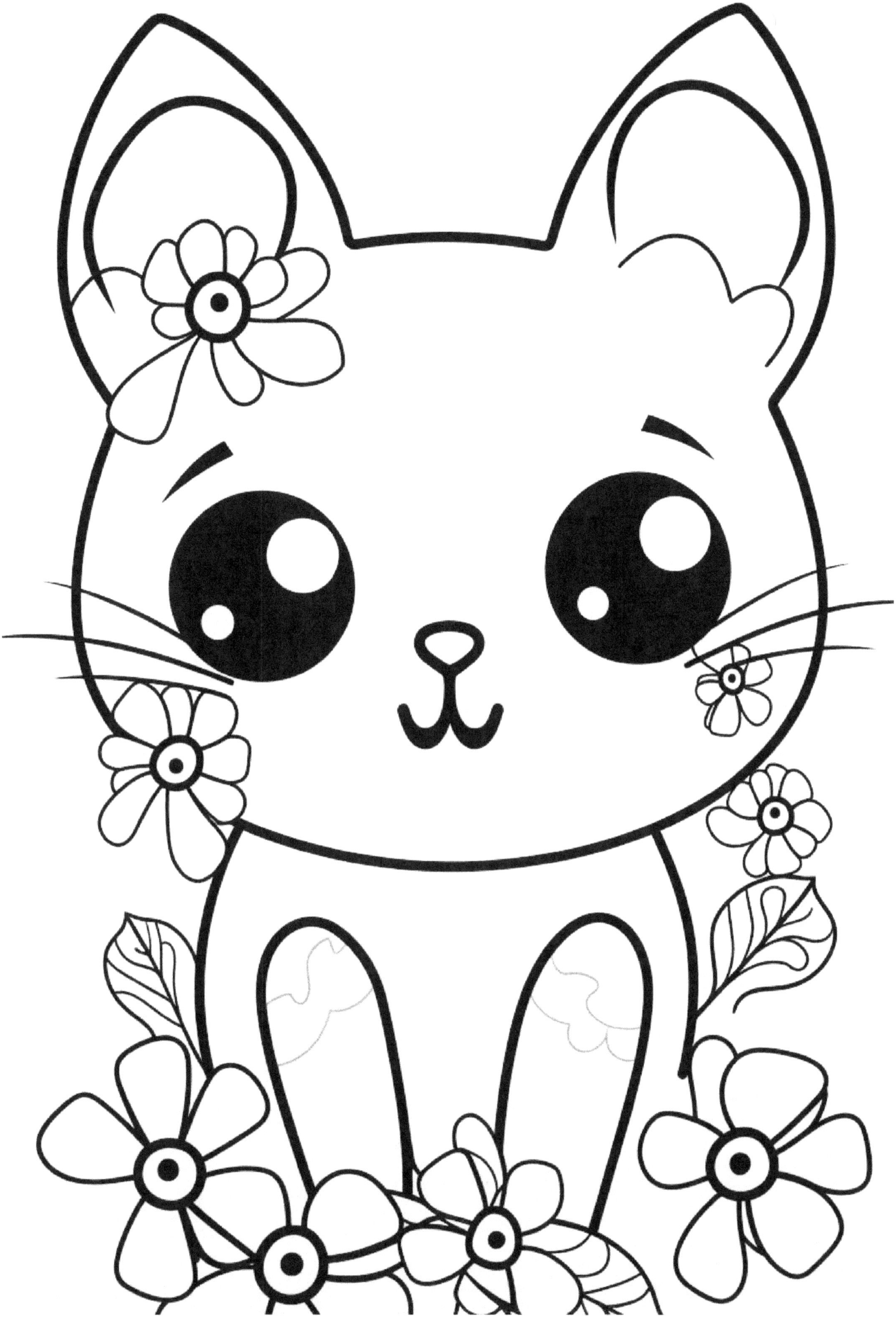

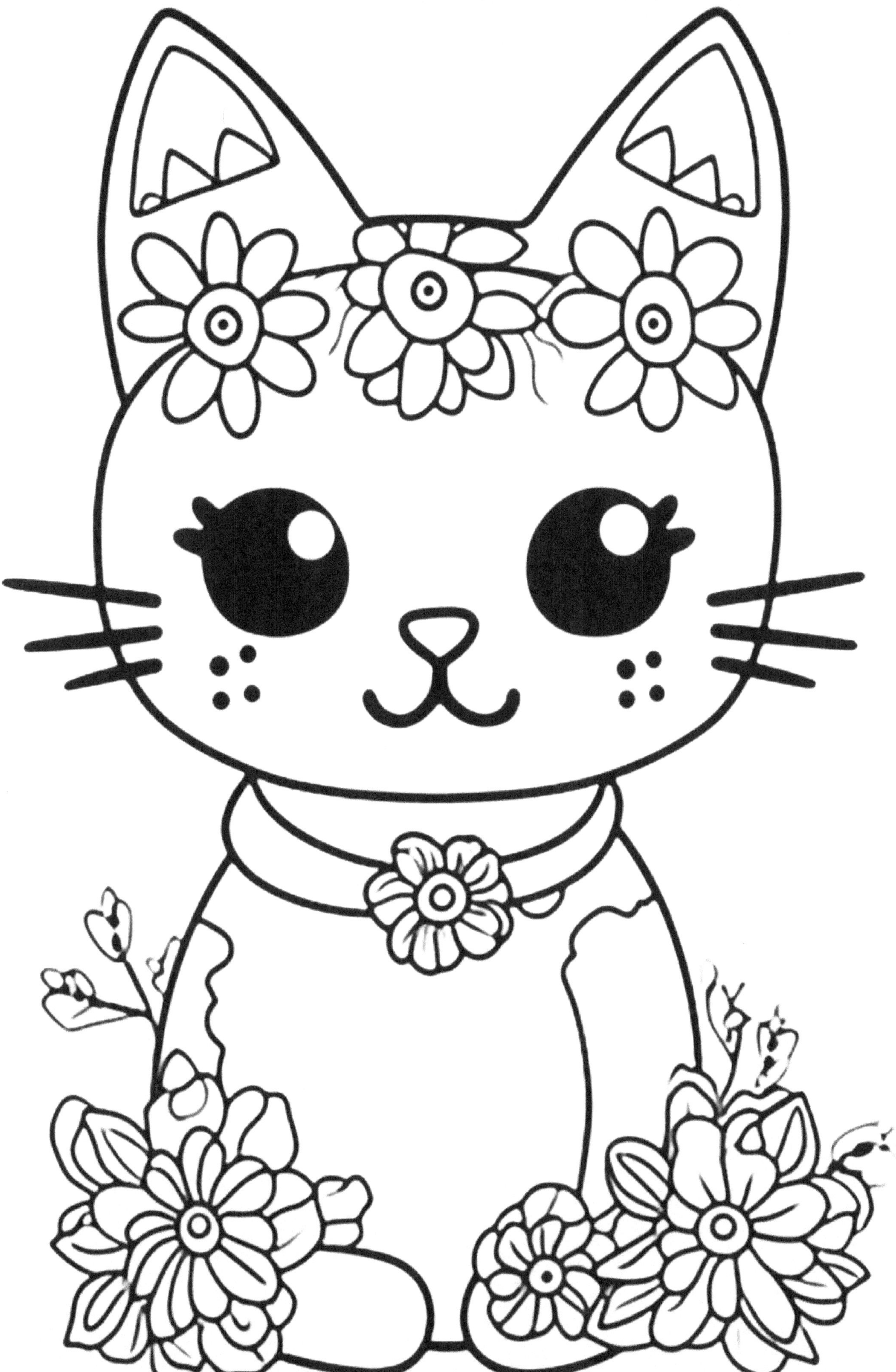

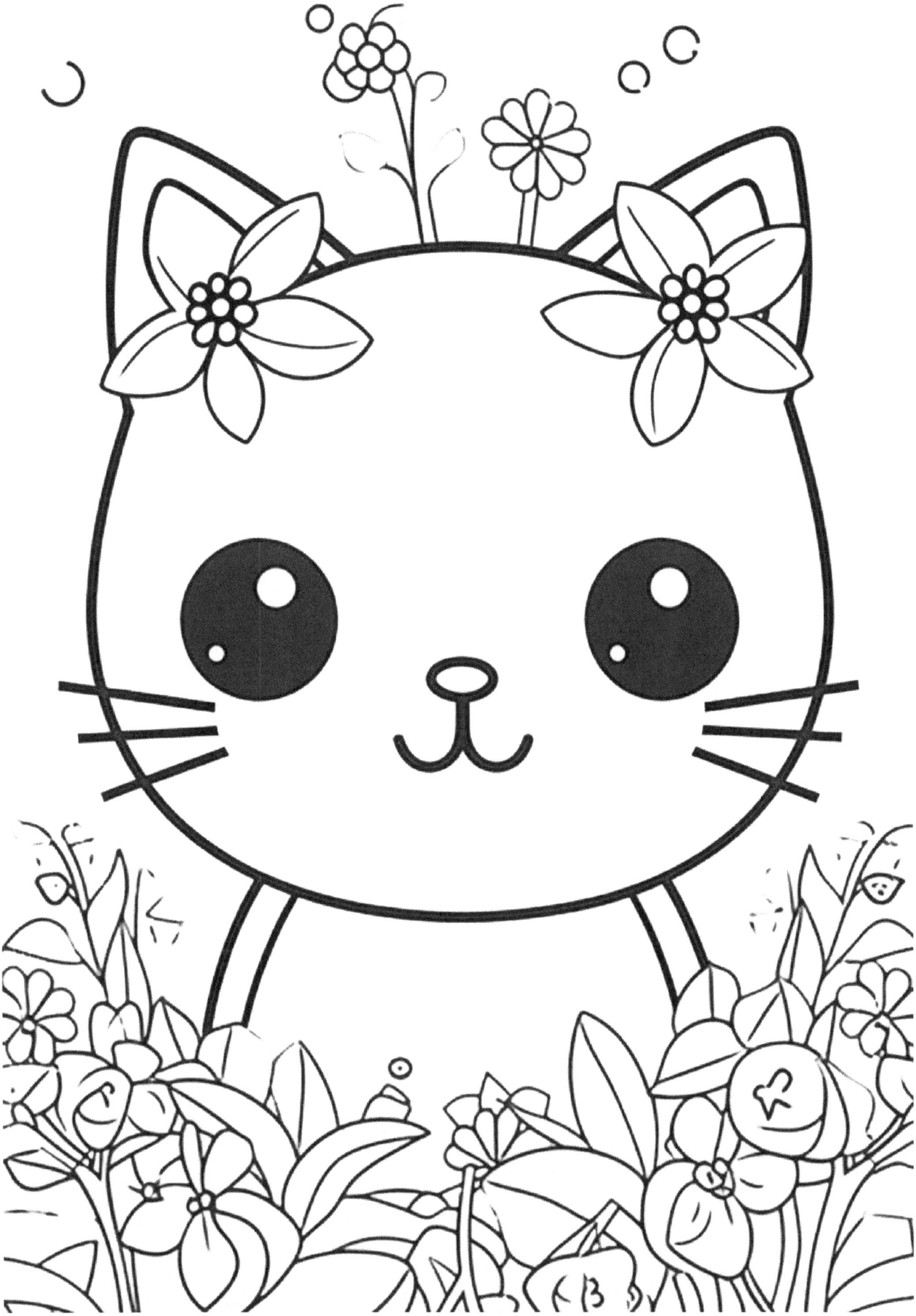

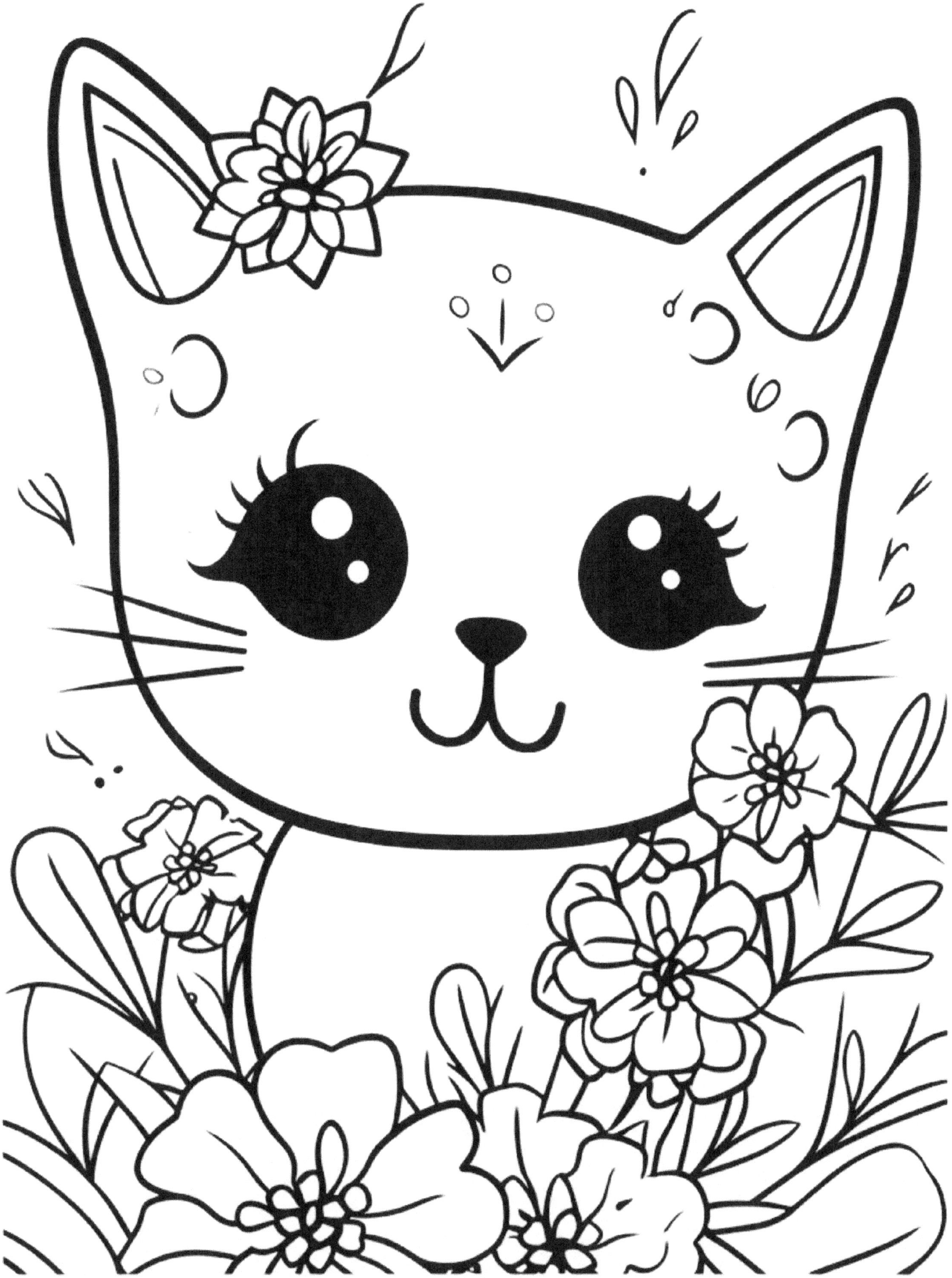

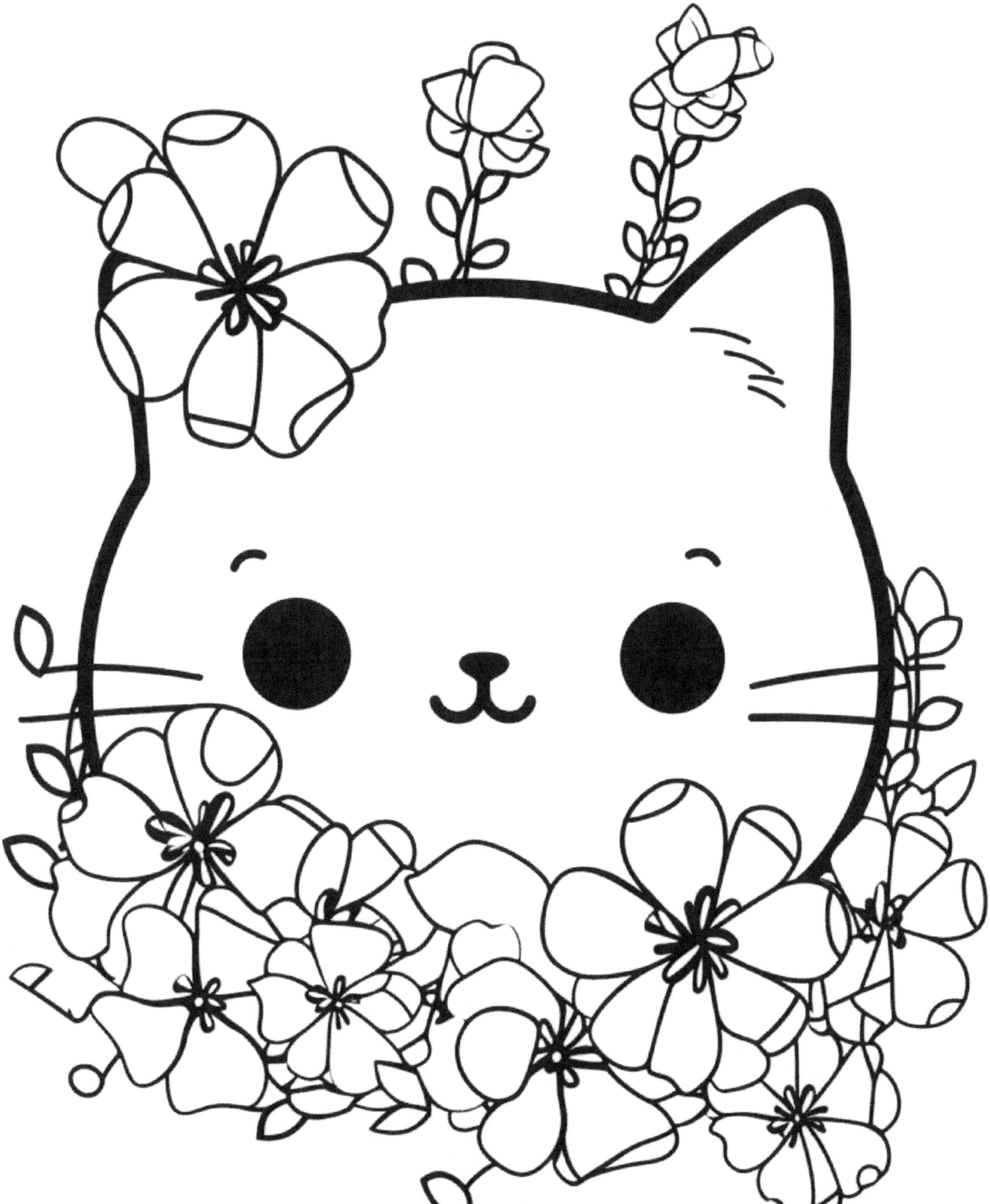

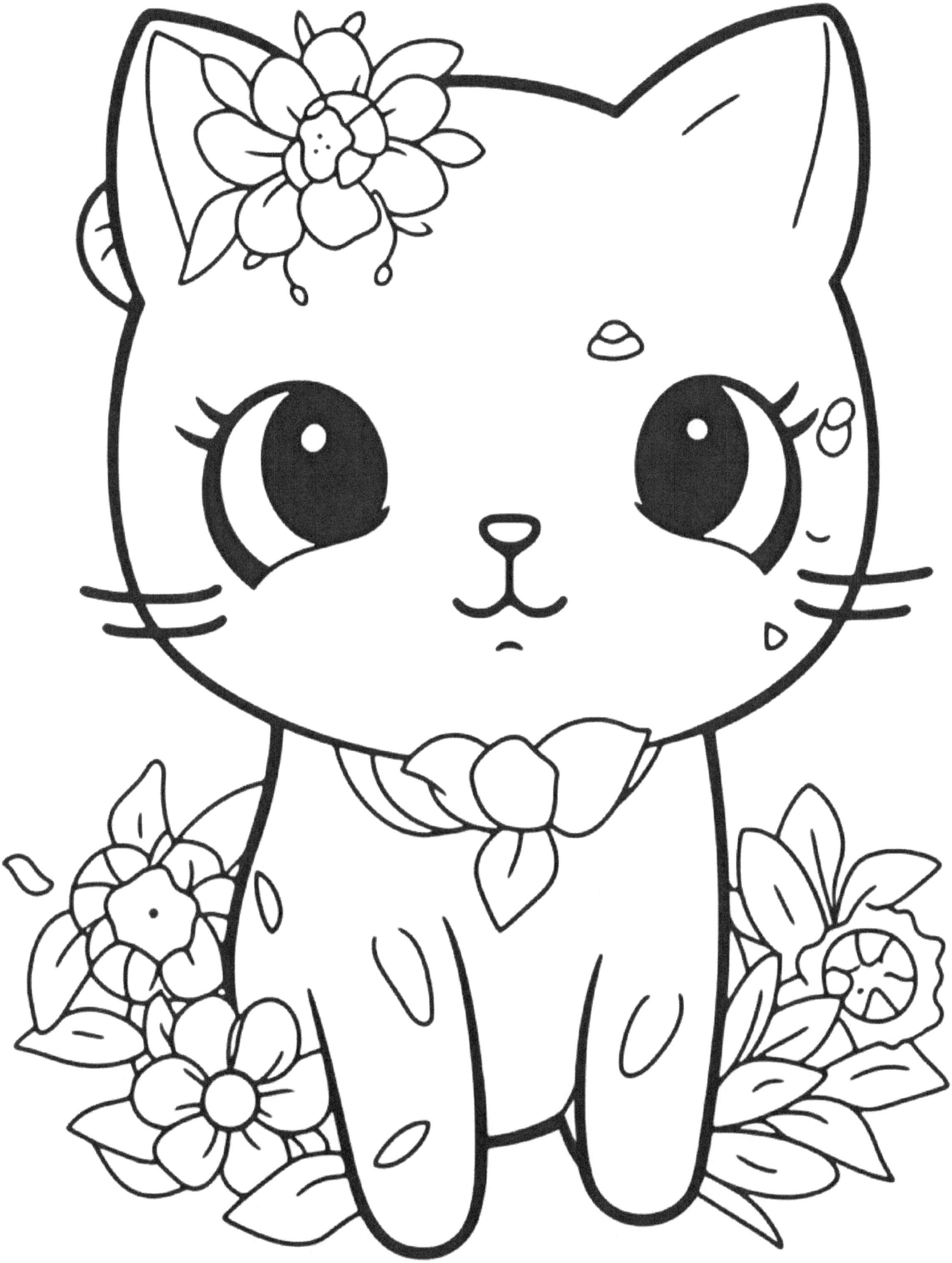

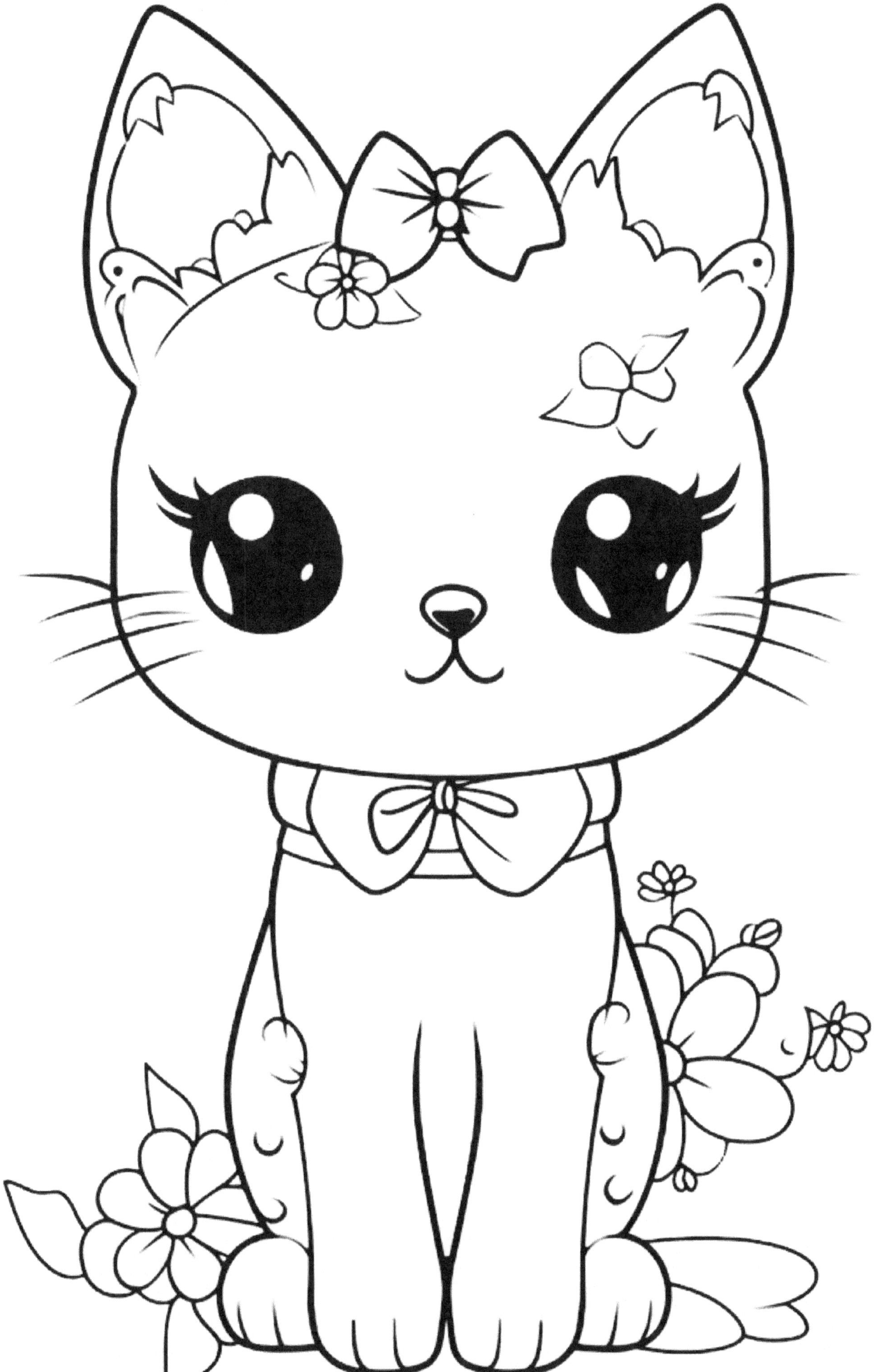

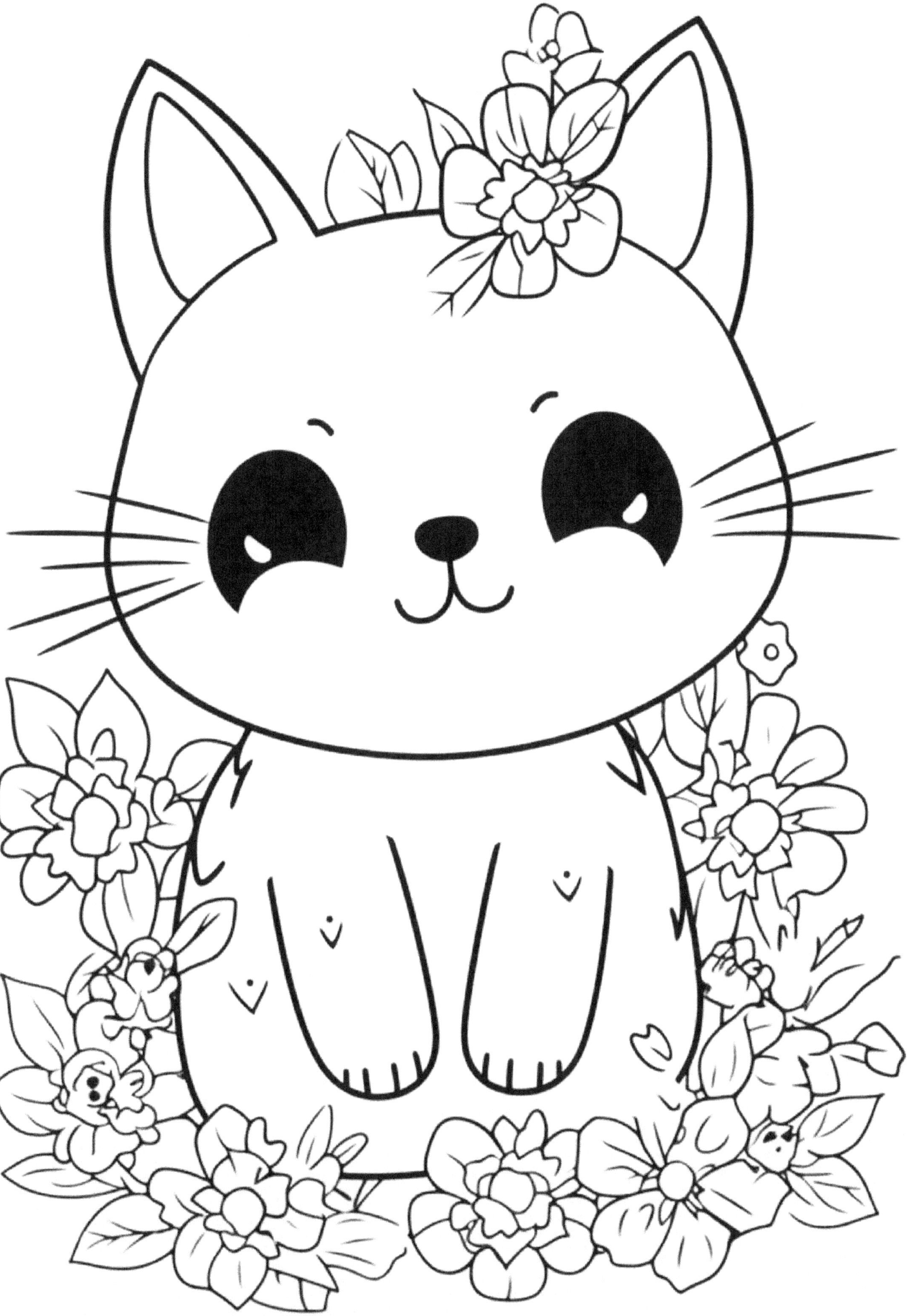

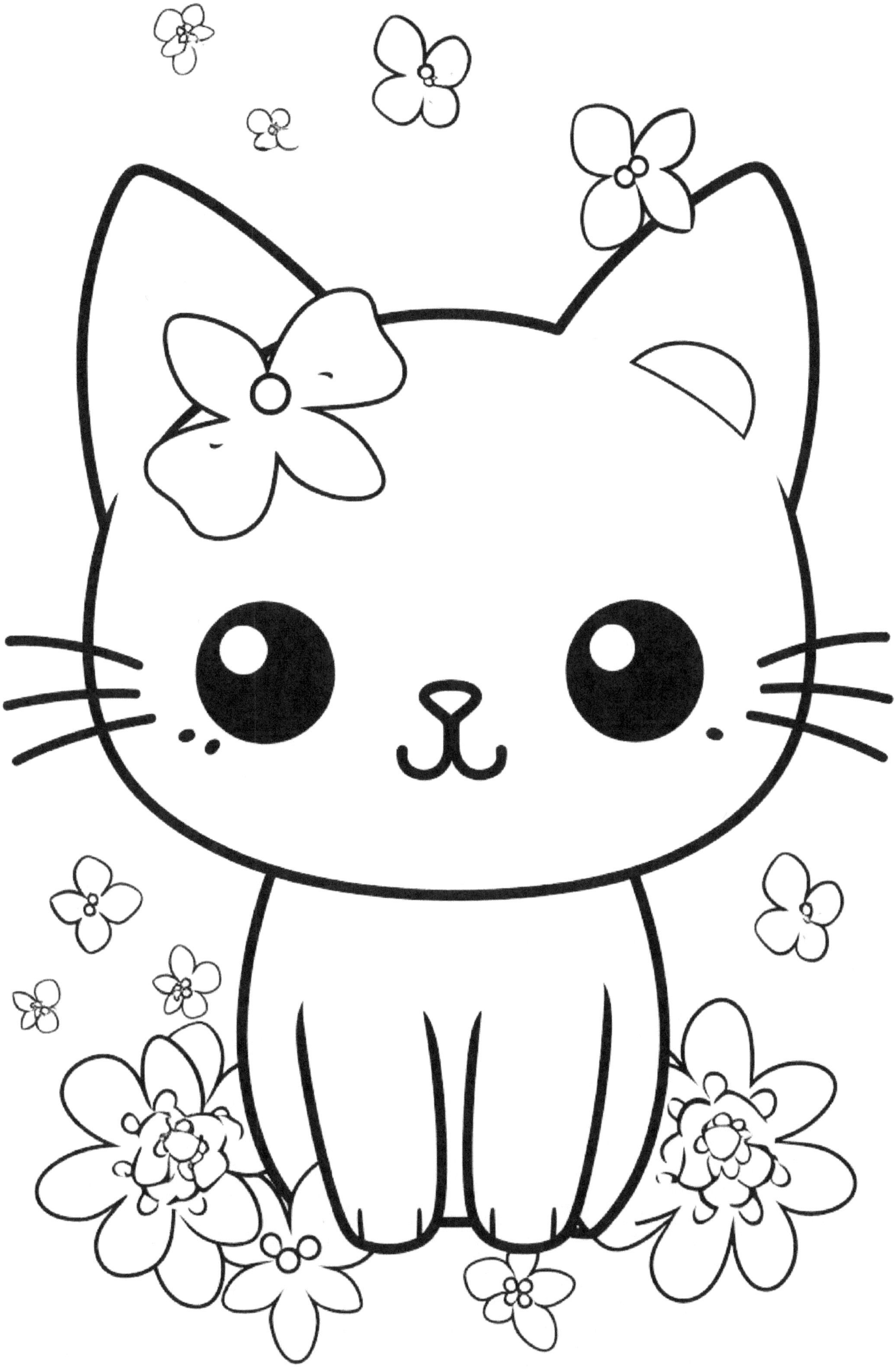

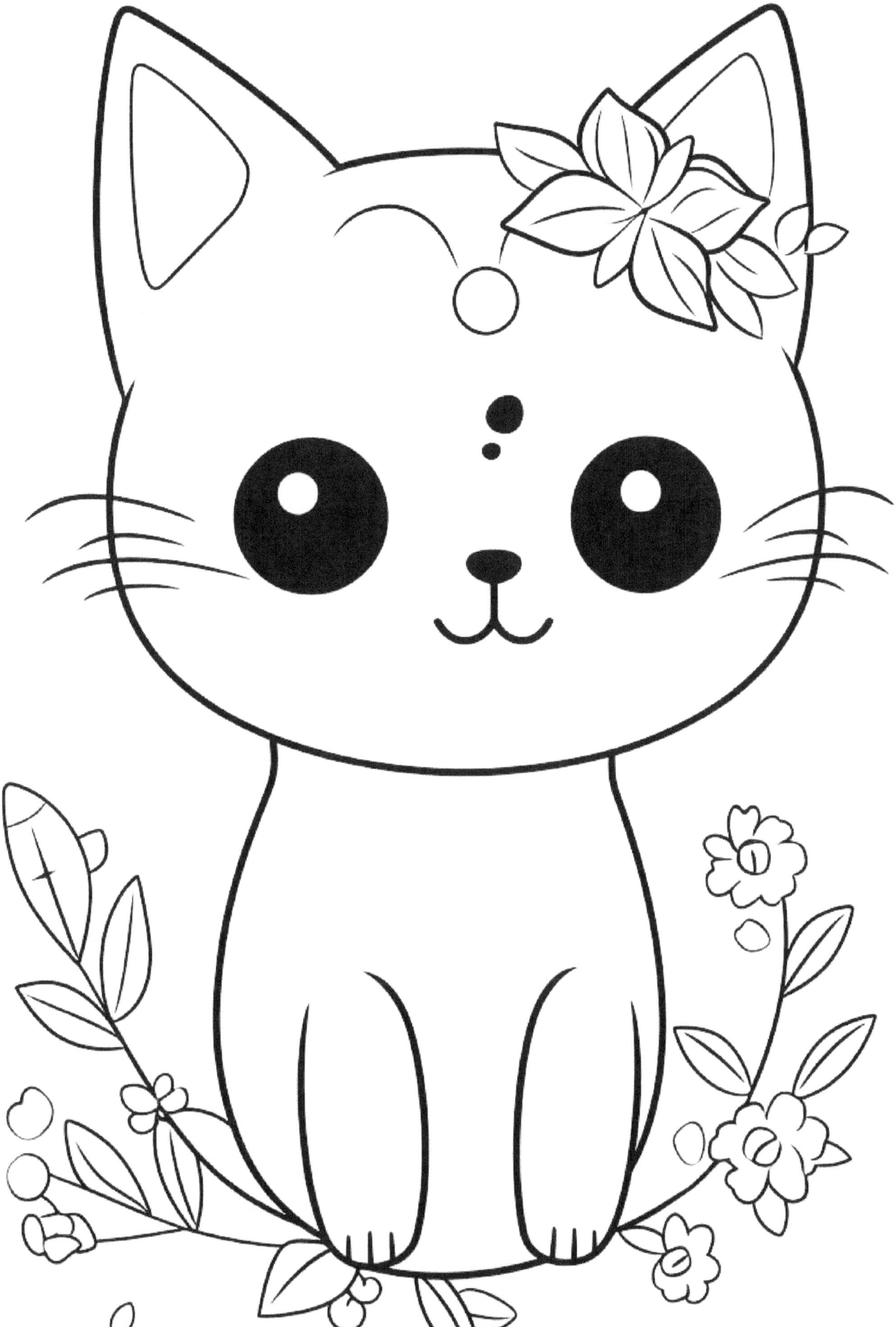

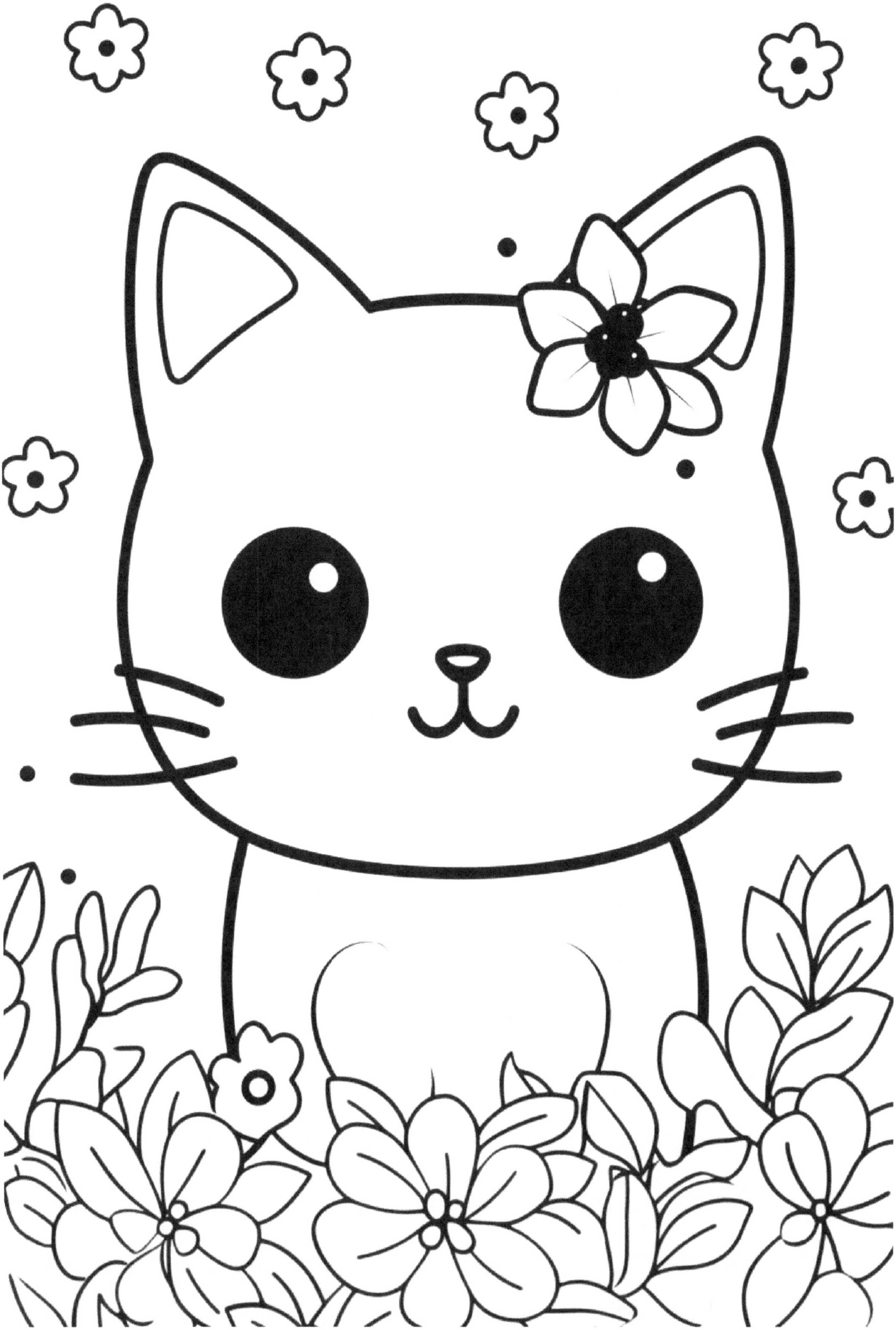

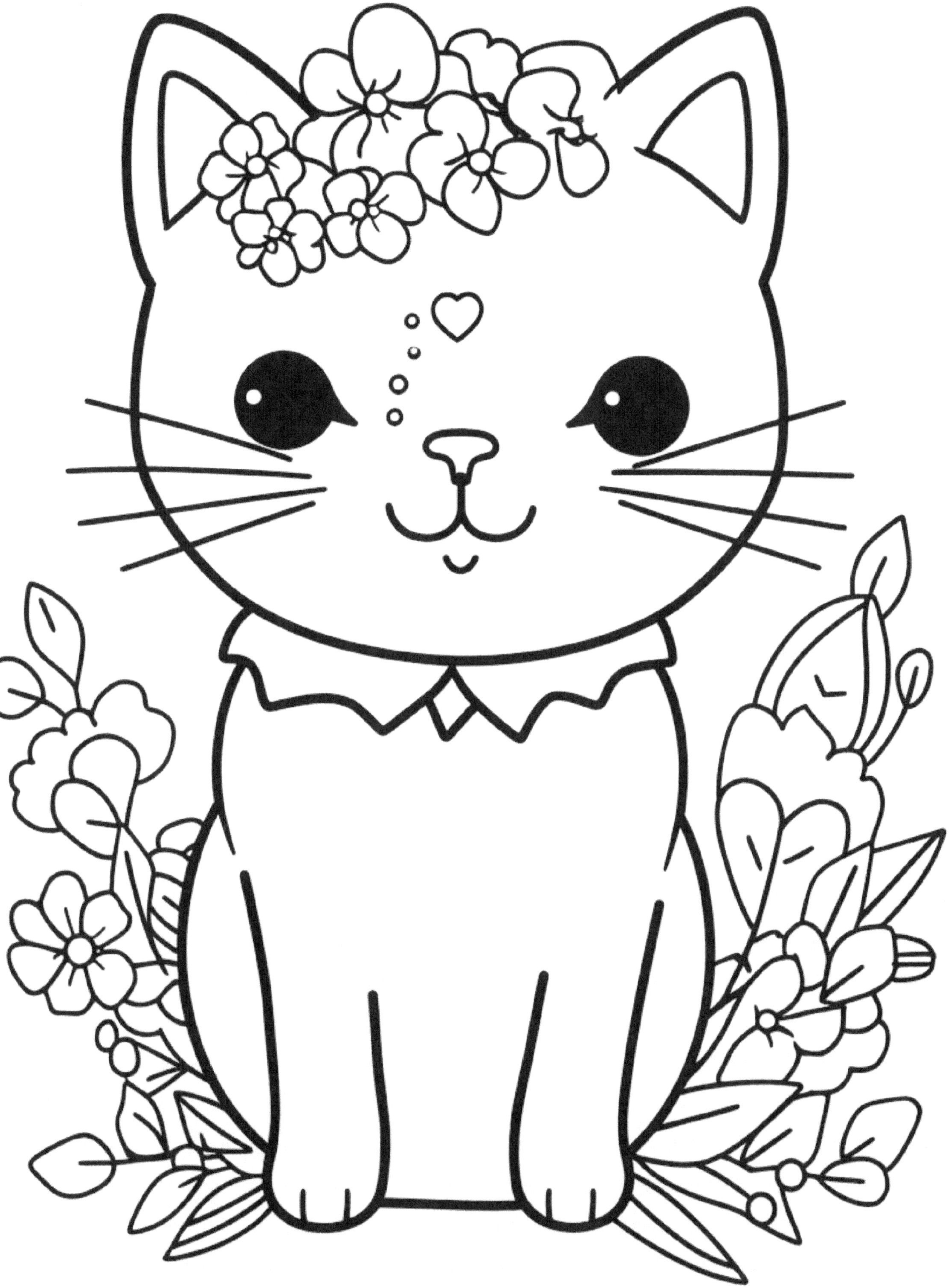

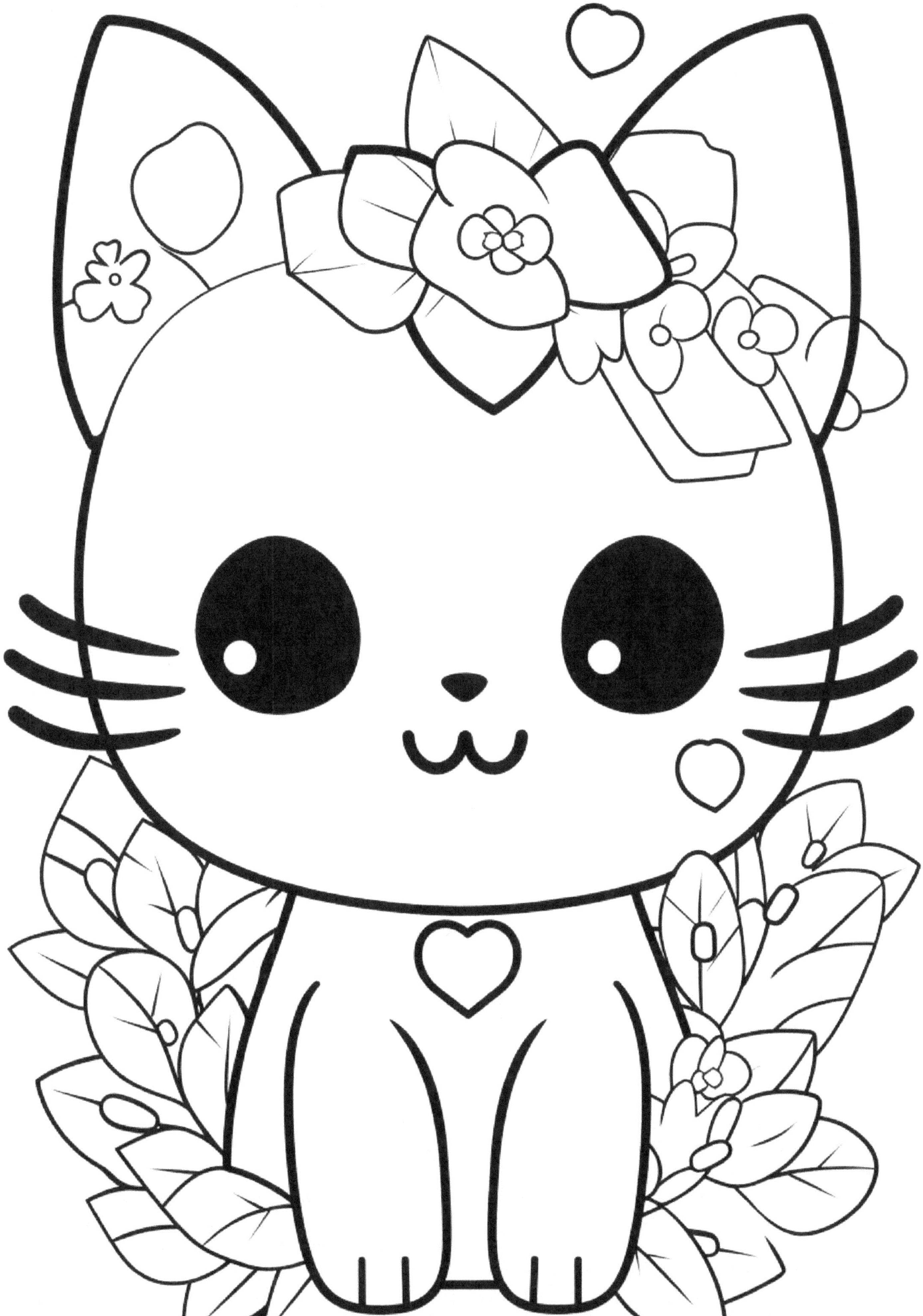

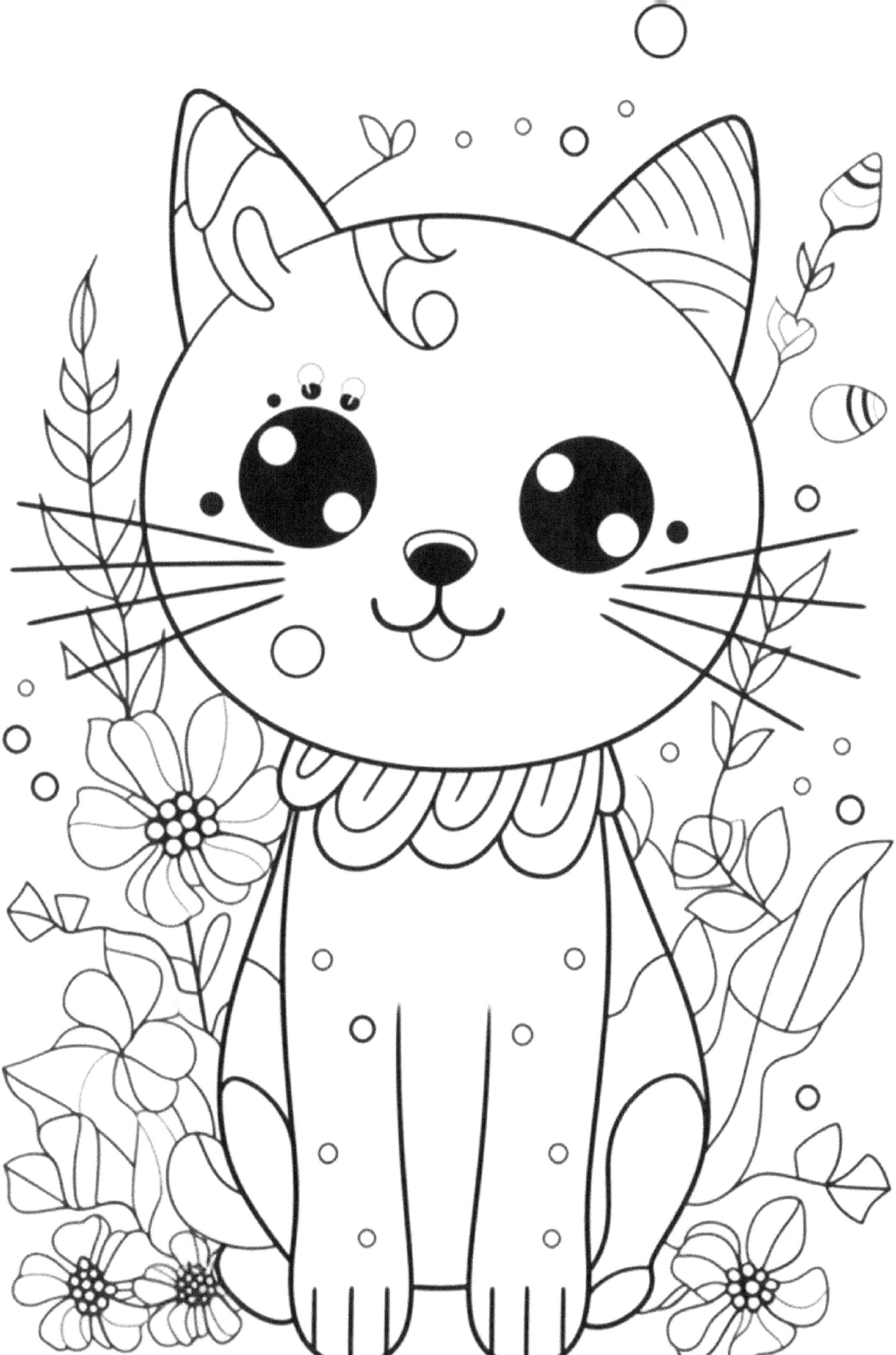

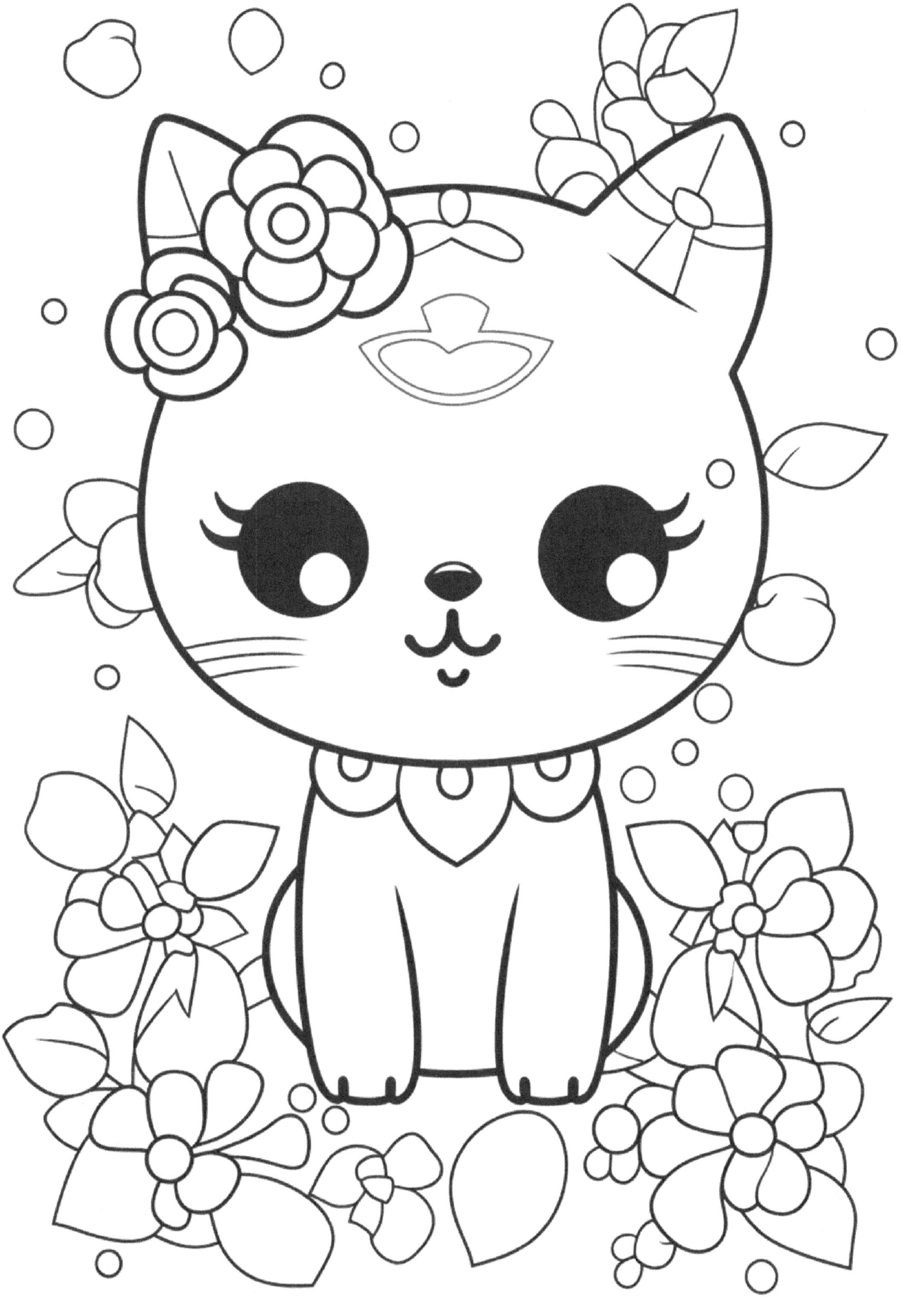

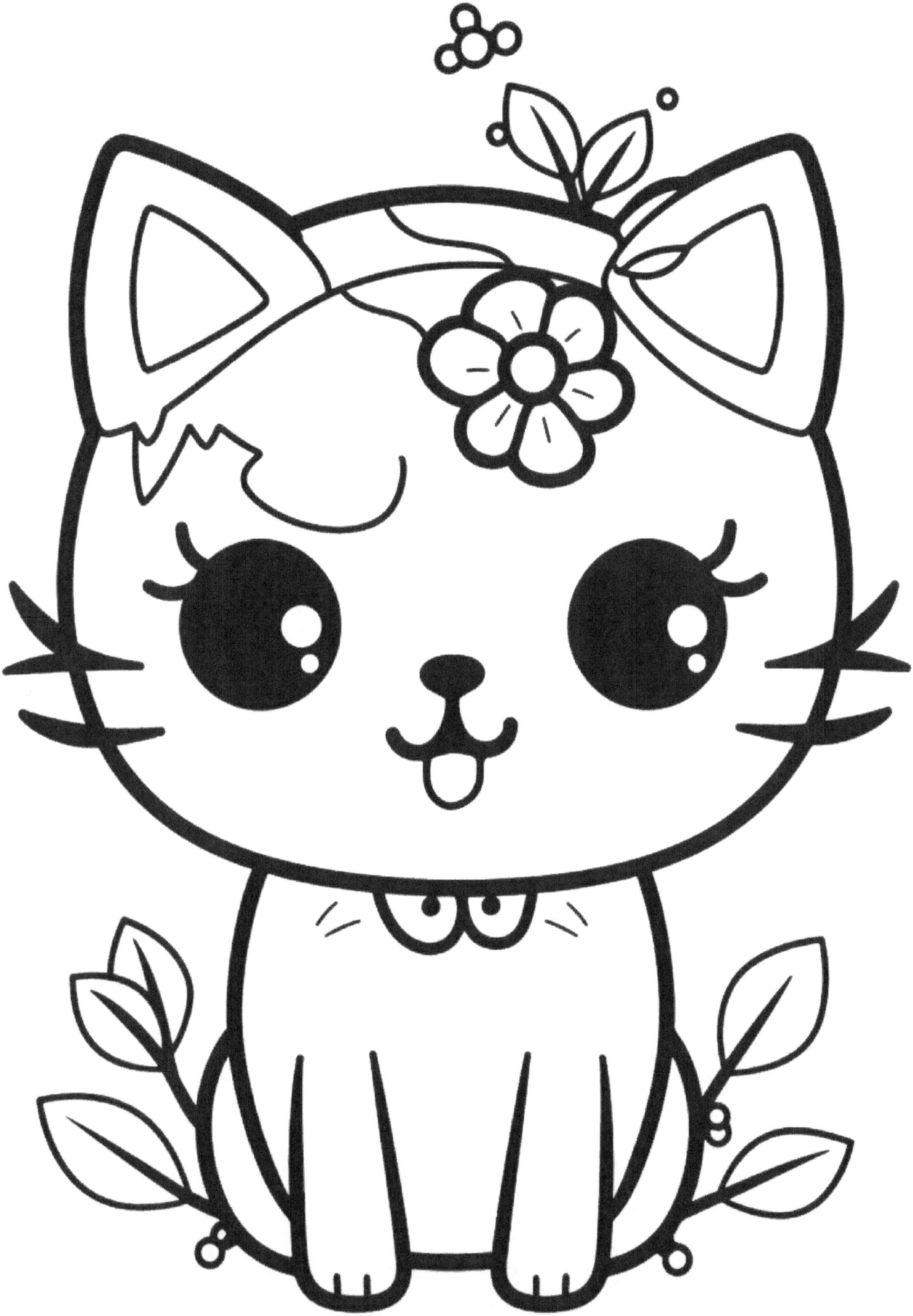

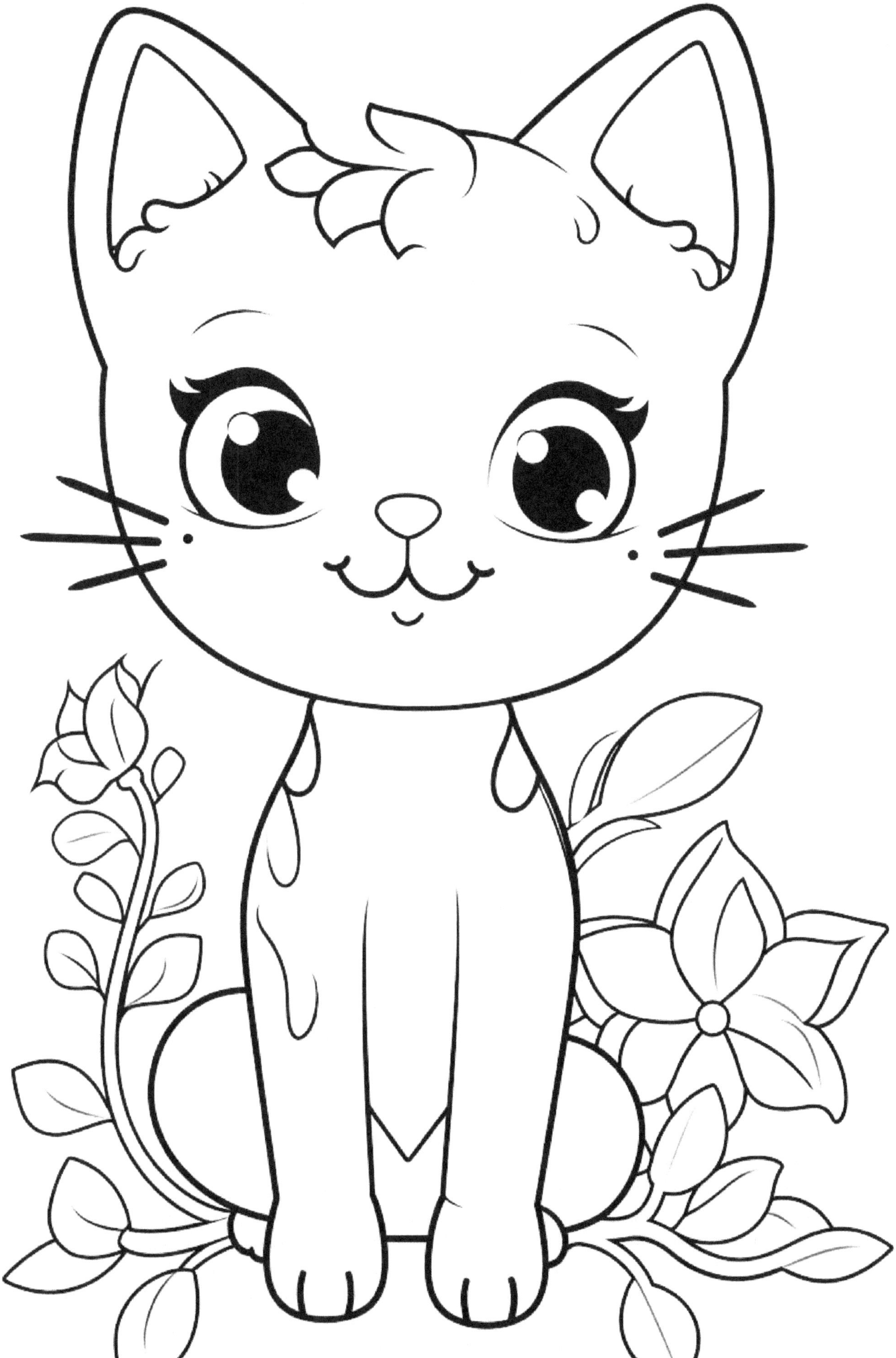

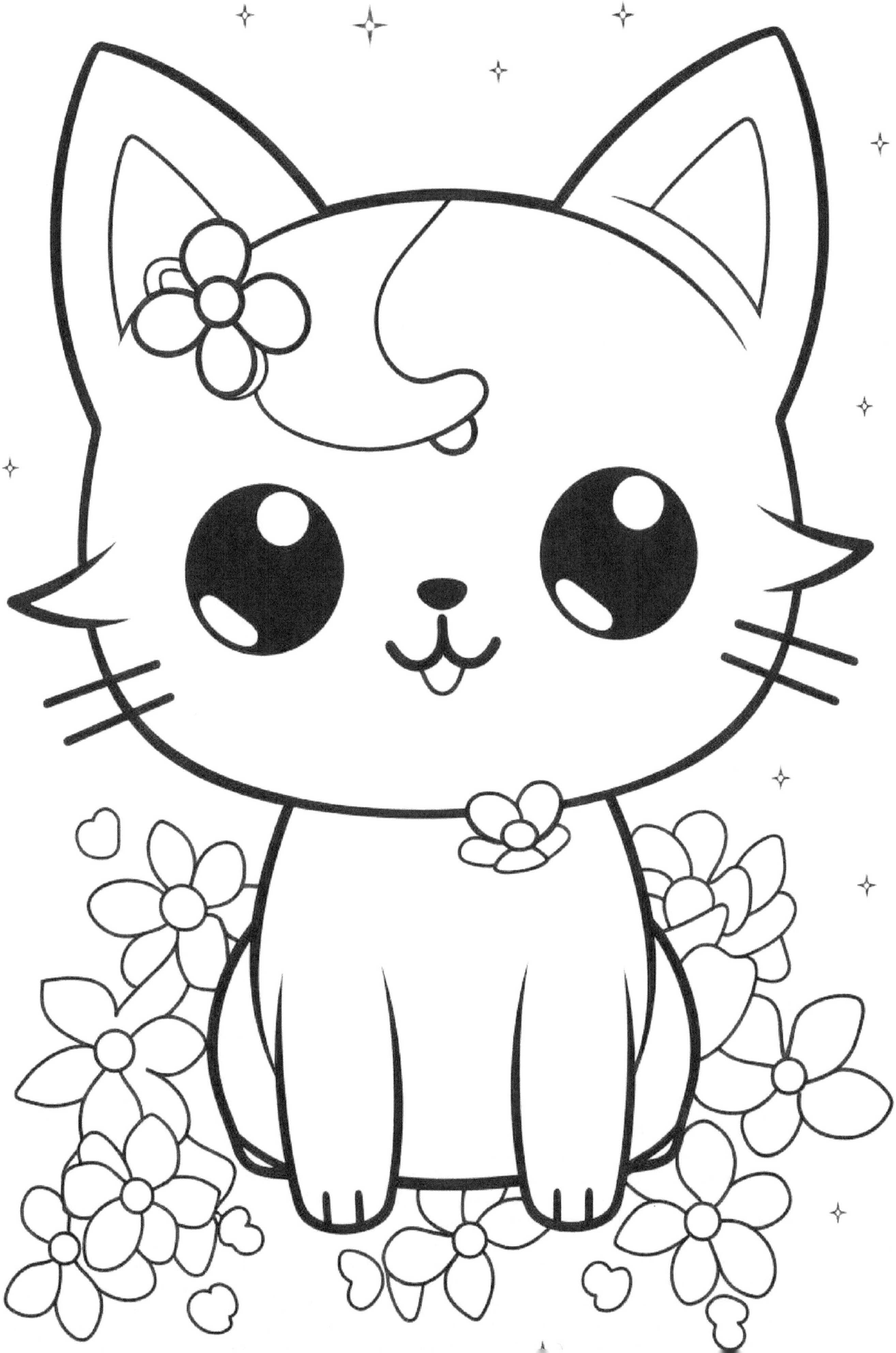

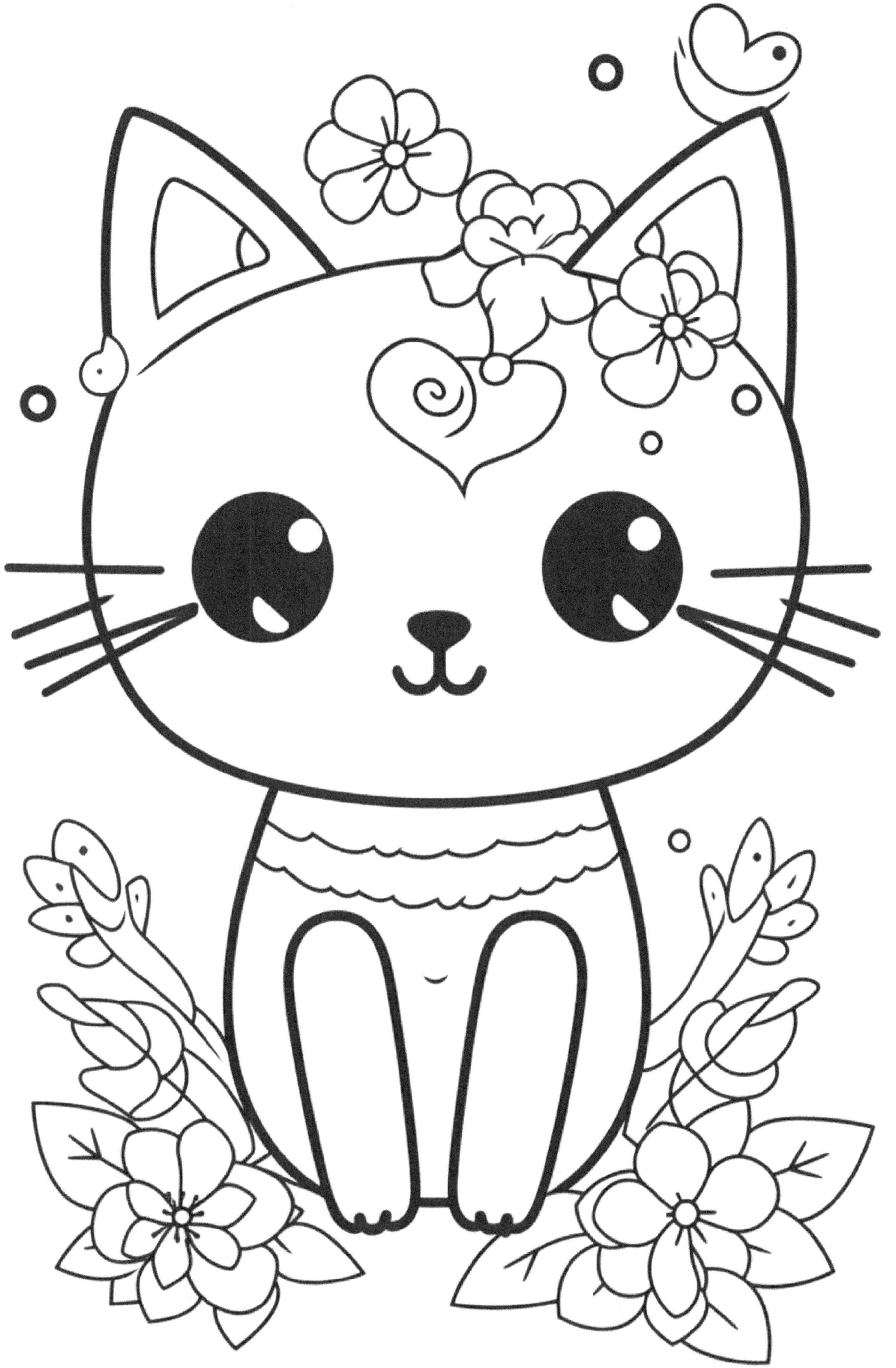

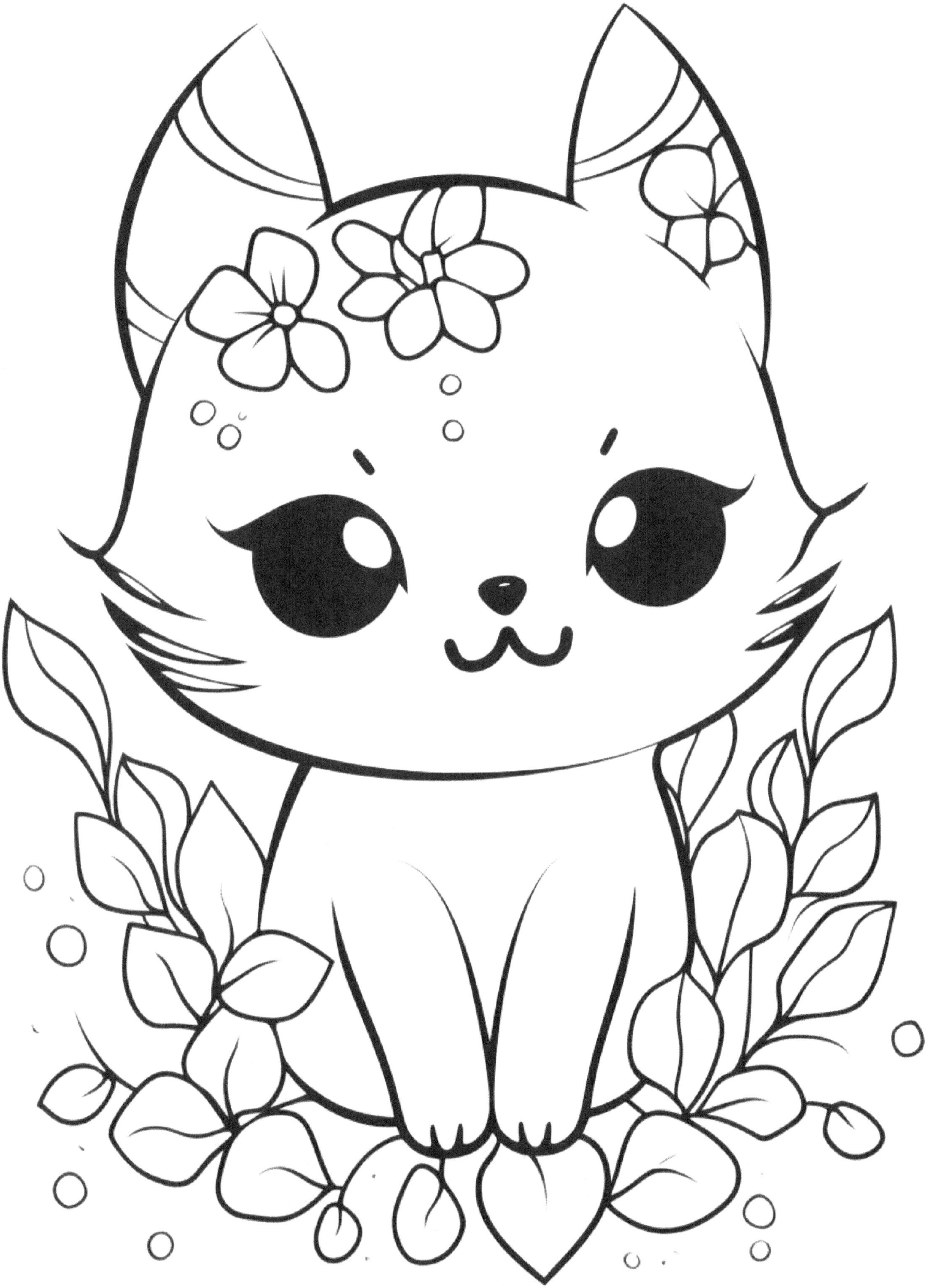

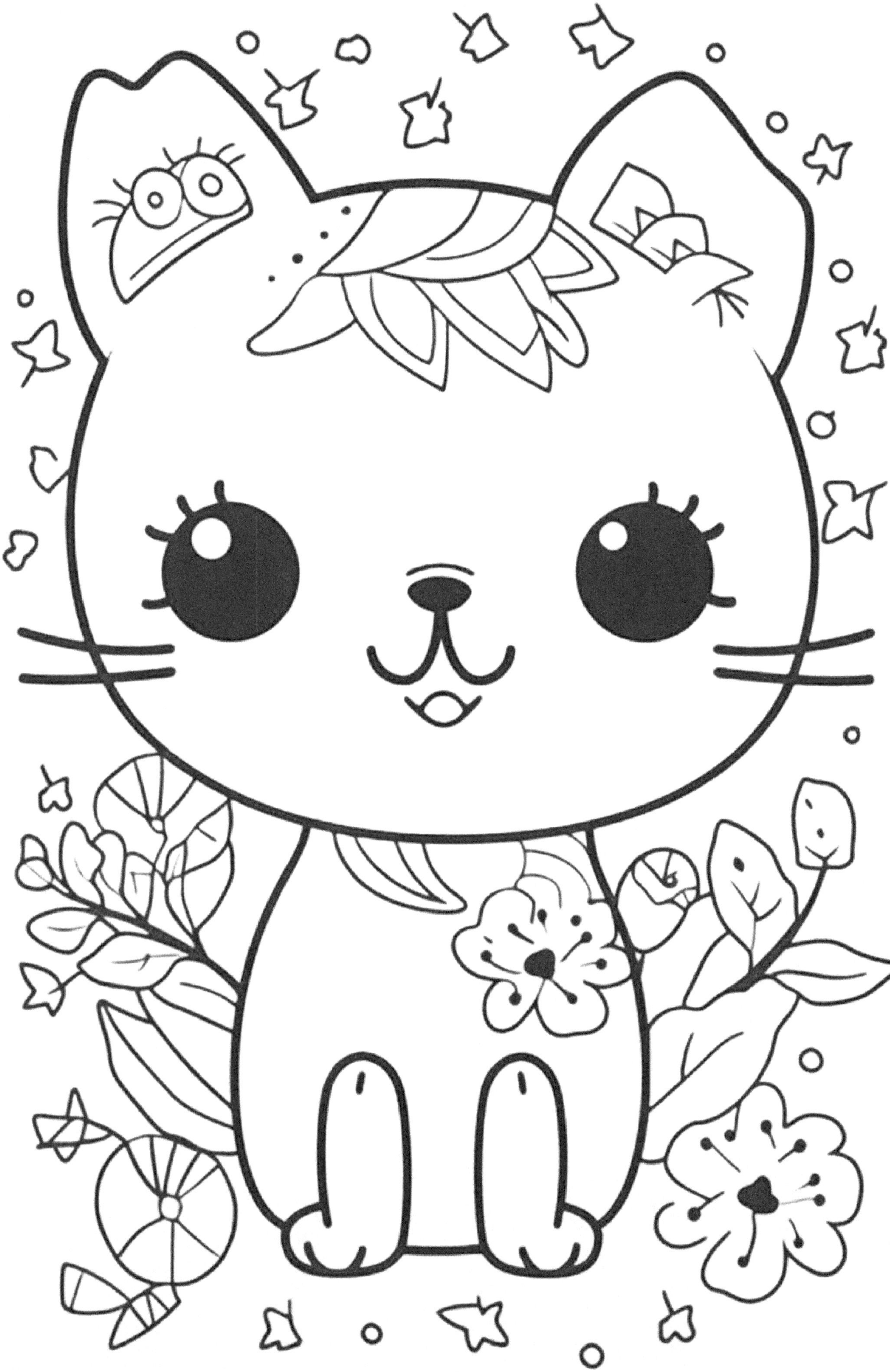

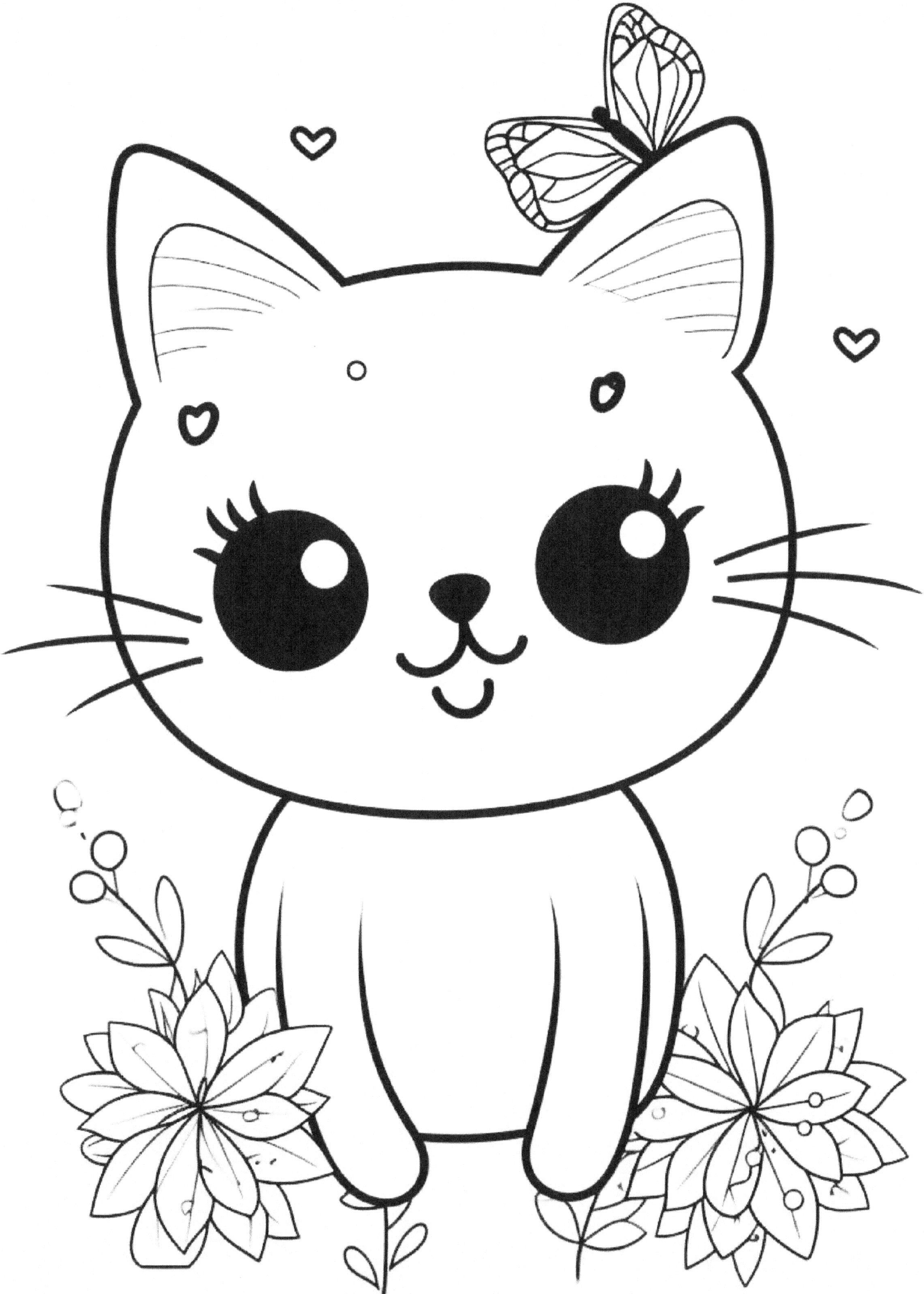

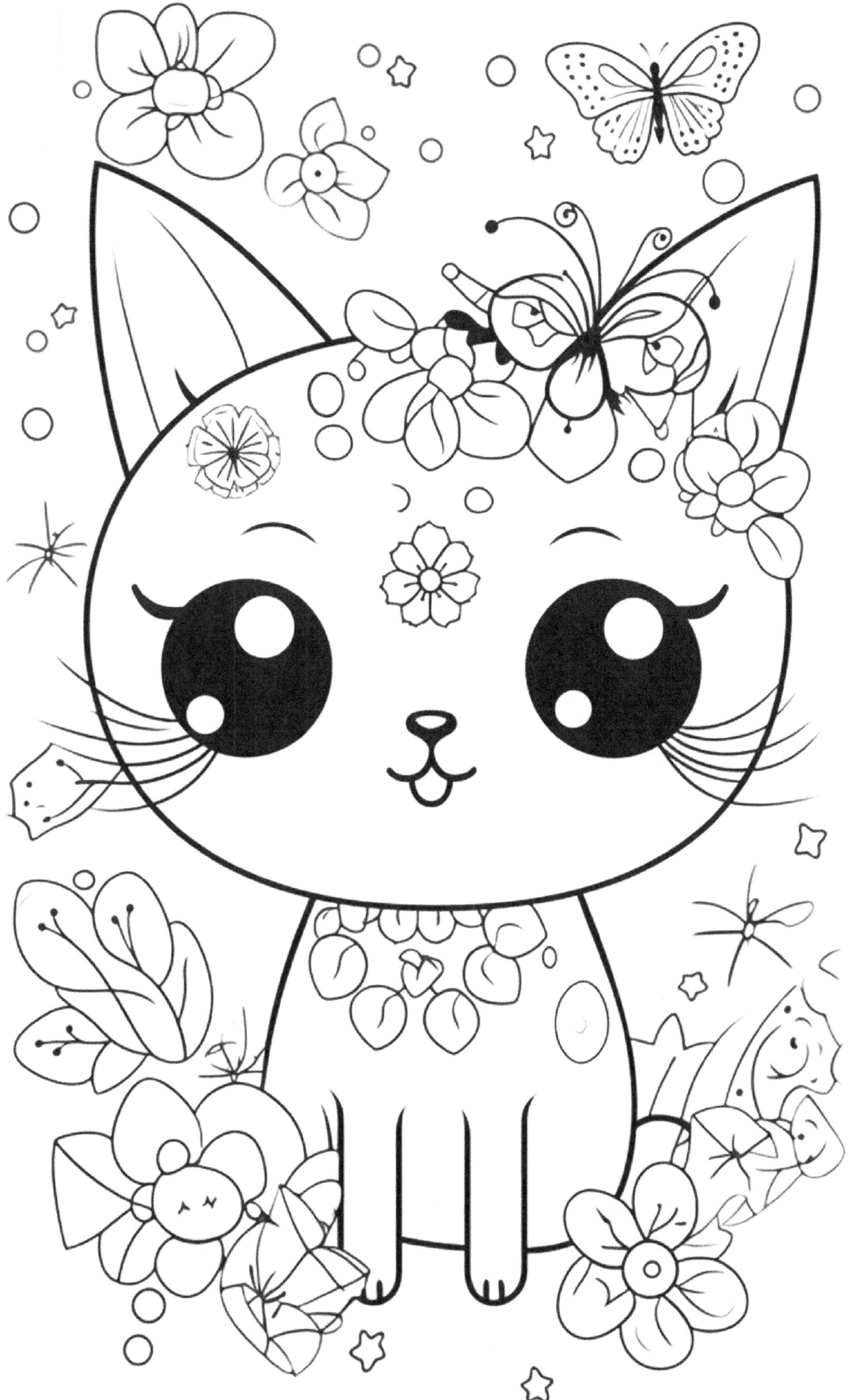

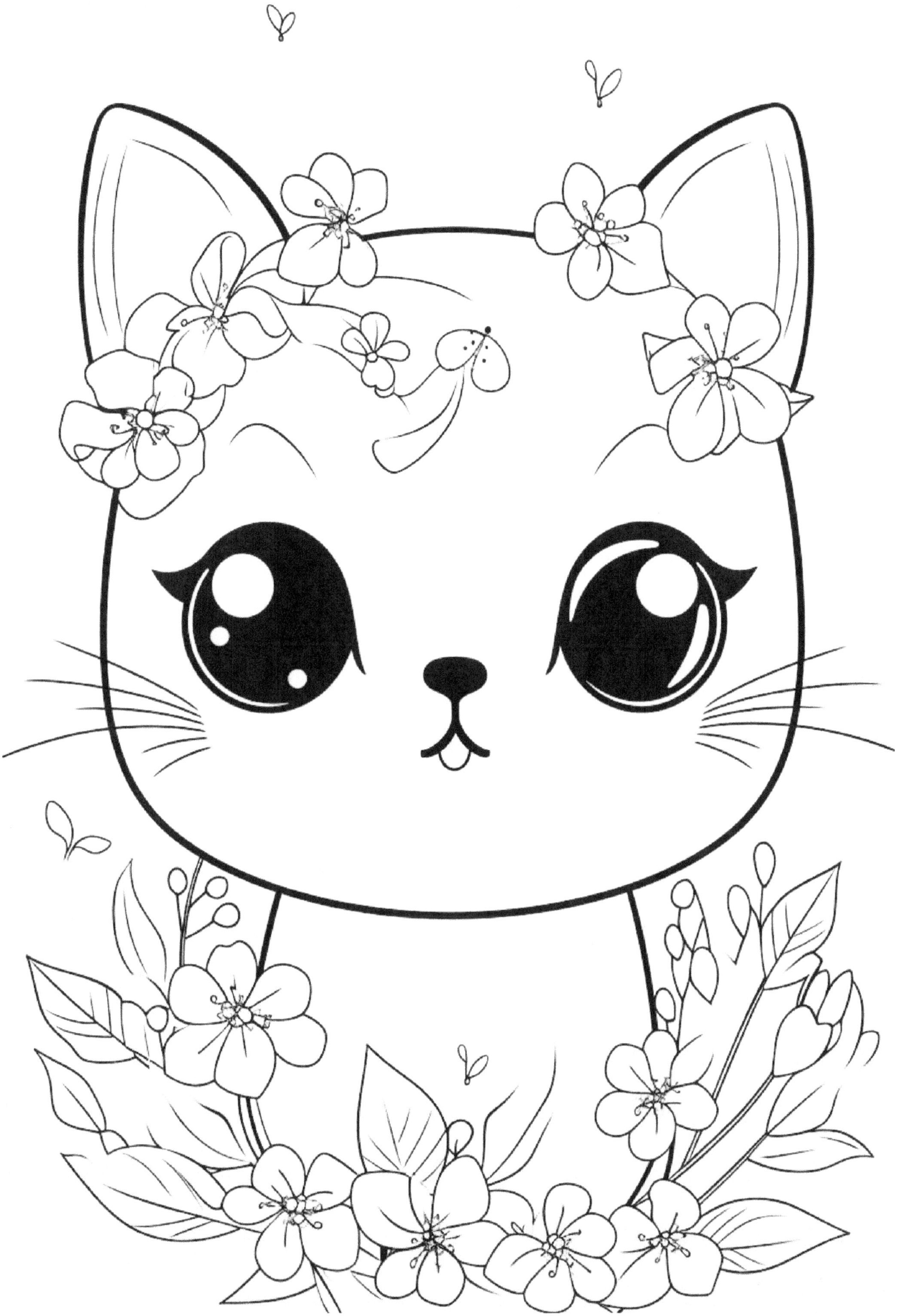

www.ingramcontent.com/pod-product-compliance
Lightning Source LLC
Chambersburg PA
CBHW082024230526
45466CB00023B/3359
* 9 7 9 8 3 9 6 2 6 5 5 3 0 *